5337
9.95
(Mil)
TPM
(Mil)

The Economics of Public Issues

Eighth Edition

The Economics of Public Issues

Roger LeRoy Miller
Clemson University

Daniel K. Benjamin
Clemson University

Douglass C. North
Washington University, St. Louis

1817

Harper & Row, Publishers, New York
Grand Rapids, Philadelphia, St. Louis, San Francisco
London, Singapore, Sydney, Tokyo

Sponsoring Editor: **John Greenman**
Project Coordination and Text Design: **R. David Newcomer Associates**
Cover Design: **Teresa J. Delgado**
Production: **Beth Maglione**

The Economics of Public Issues, Eighth Edition

Library of Congress Cataloging-in-Publication Data

Miller, Roger LeRoy.
    The economics of public issues / Roger LeRoy Miller, Daniel K.
Benjamin, Douglass C. North. — 8th ed.
        p.   cm.
    North's name appears first on the earlier edition.
    ISBN 0-06-044850-4
    1. Economics.   2. Industry and state.   3. Economic policy.
I. Benjamin, Daniel K.   II. North, Douglass Cecil.   III. Title.
HB34.N6   1990
330.973'092—dc20   89-26997
                                                              CIP

90 91 92 93   9 8 7 6 5 4 3 2 1

Col. B 5337 /9. 95 9.91

R.L.M. dedicates this edition to Ian Gowrie-Smith,
a friend always.

D.K.B. dedicates this edition to Danny and Jessica,
who could have written it themselves,
if they had taken notes at dinner.

Contents

Preface   *ix*

Part One

Supply and Demand   *1*

1   Sex, Booze, and Drugs   *3*
2   Pity the Poor Farmer—All the Way to the Bank   *13*
3   Raising the Minimum Wage   *20*
4   Water, Water Everywhere, Nor Any Drop to Drink?   *25*
5   Flying the Friendly Skies?   *31*
6   Choice and Life: The Economics of Abortion   *40*

Part Two

Market Structures   *49*

7   A Random Walk Down Wall Street   *51*
8   Better Late Than Never: The Economics of
    Airline Delays   *57*
9   The Two-Edged Sword of Drug Regulation   *69*
10   Up, Up, and Away: The Rising Costs of
    Medical Care   *75*
11   International Cartels   *84*
12   Bailout at $300 Billion: The Great S&L Mess   *91*

Part Three

Factor Markets   99

13   *Women and Divorce*   101
14   *The Graying of America*   105
15   *Bankrupt Landlords, from Sea to Shining Sea*   112
16   *The Economics of Crime Prevention*   120
17   *More Taxes and Less Work*   129

Part Four

Social Issues and Externalities   133

18   *The Social Costs of Drug Wars*   135
19   *A Farewell to Elephants: The Economics of Extinction*   144
20   *Oil Pollution, Obvious and Otherwise*   151
21   *Clamming and Other "Free" Goods*   157
22   *Bubbleology: The Economics of Selling Pollution*   162
23   *Crime and Punishment*   168

Part Five

Political Economy   177

24   *Killing the American Dream: Government Regulation
     and the High Price of Houses*   179
25   *Ecology and Income Distribution*   185
26   *Waging War on Poverty*   190
27   *The Changing Face of Poverty*   198
28   *Education and Choice: The Economics of Schools*   206
29   *Income Distribution and Government Programs*   214
30   *Where There's Smoking, There's Fire*   219

     Glossary of Terms   224
     Index   233

Preface

Economists cannot tell people what they ought to do. They can only expose the costs and benefits of various alternatives so that citizens in a democratic society can make better choices. In this book, we present the interested reader with some ideas of what the costs and benefits are for various proposed social actions. Economic issues surround us in our daily lives, in our work, and in our play. Often, we may not even be aware of the extent to which economics affects public issues. Nonetheless, it plays a large role in most public issues, whether we are talking about water, illegal drugs, crime prevention, higher education, or poverty.

For students taking an introductory economics course, this book is offered as a supplement to the main text. Reading it in conjunction with a book that explains economic theory in detail can demonstrate both the relevance of that theory and the way in which it can be used to analyze the world around us. No previously acquired knowledge of economics is necessary to understand any of the chapters in this book. Necessarily, then, the reader must be warned that in no case is our treatment of a topic exhaustive. We have merely attempted to expose the bare economic bones of some aspects of the issues treated. Further class discussion will undoubtedly reveal the more complex nature of those issues.

Long-time users of *The Economics of Public Issues* will notice a virtually new book. With the addition of a new co-author we decided to attack the analysis of public issues essentially *de novo*. Nineteen out of the 30 chapters are either new or completely revised. The remainder have, of course, been updated.

First-time users of *The Economics of Public Issues* will find the most important social issues of the day discussed. We haven't shied away from controversial issues. Indeed, we think students can be most excited by economics if the topics discussed in class are controversial. One is bound to get diverse views when students read Chapter 1 on sex, drugs, and booze or Chapter 6 on the economics of abortion. Students may sit up in their chairs when they discover in Chapter 12 how much the savings and loan bailout is costing each and every one of them in implicit future taxes. Some will certainly have an opinion or two to voice when they read Chapter 18 on the social costs of America's war on drugs.

Our goal has always been, and continues to be, to present different sides of today's important world issues. Teaching economic theory by way of current issues continues to prove effective for many instructors. The new issues that we have chosen will continue, we believe, to keep students interested in microeconomic analysis.

This book includes the following set of pedagogical devices to help the student reader better understand the economic analysis that applies to each part and chapter:

1. An introductory explanation precedes each of the five parts. Where applicable, economic terms are set in boldface in these introductions.
2. Economic terms are set in boldface the first time they appear in the text. All these boldface terms are defined in the glossary at the end of the text.
3. Each chapter ends with discussion questions suitable for classroom use.

Through the years, many instructors have given us ideas, suggestions, and criticisms. For the most recent editions, we were able to obtain the helpful written comments of the following reviewers: Richard V. Burkhauser, Vanderbilt University; Eleanor Craig, University of Delaware; John H. Haehl, California State University at Fullerton; Bassam Harik, Western Michigan University; David Easley, Cornell University; Ashley Lyman, University of Idaho; James McLain, University of New Orleans; Michael K. Mischaikow, Western Washington University; Gaston V. Rimlinger, Rice University; and Marcia Frost Watkins, Pepperdine University. To these reviewers, we wish to express our sincere appreciation for their numerous helpful comments. As always, we take responsibility for any remaining errors. We continue to welcome all comments and suggestions for change.

Roger LeRoy Miller
Daniel K. Benjamin
Douglass C. North

The Economics
of Public Issues

Part One

Supply
and Demand

INTRODUCTION

Supply and demand analysis forms the basis of virtually all economic analysis. In this part, we look at a number of issues, some of which do not appear to lend themselves to economic analysis. Nonetheless, each and every issue does, in fact, have an economic aspect. As you read about illicit drugs, agricultural products, **minimum wages**, and water, for example, you will find that supply and demand analysis applies throughout.

While reading about these issues, keep in mind the following:

1. The **law of demand** and the **law of supply** are given, holding other things constant.
2. A change in price affects quantities demanded and supplied. A change in any other nonprice variable shifts the entire demand or supply curve; in other words, there is a clear distinction between quantity demanded and supplied and demand and supply.
3. The laws of supply and demand relate price per **constant quality unit** to quantities supplied and demanded.

It is not necessary for everyone to react to price changes for the laws of demand and supply to be valid; the only requirement is that *some* marginal buyers or marginal producers react to price changes. In economics, all movement is on the margin.

1

Sex, Booze, and Drugs

Prior to 1914, cocaine was legal in this country; today it is not. Alcohol (of the intoxicating variety) is legal in America today; from 1920 to 1933 it was not. Prostitution is legal in Nevada today; in the other 49 states it is not.[1] All three of these goods—sex, booze, and drugs—share at least one property: The consumption of each brings together a willing seller with a willing buyer; there is an act of "mutually beneficial exchange" (at least from the perspective of the parties involved). Partly because of this property, past and present attempts to

---

[1]As the sticklers in the crowd will note, these statements are not *quite* correct. Even today, cocaine may be legally obtained by prescription from a physician. Prostitution in Nevada is legal only in those counties that have, by virtue of "local option," chosen to proclaim it as such. Finally, some counties in the U.S. remain "dry," prohibiting the sale of beer, wine, and distilled spirits.

proscribe the consumption of these goods have (1) met with less than spectacular success, and (2) yielded some peculiar patterns of production, distribution, and usage. Let's see why.

When the government tries to prevent voluntary exchange, it generally has to decide whether to go after the seller or the buyer. In most cases—and certainly when sex, booze, or drugs have been involved—the government cracks down most heavily on sellers, because this is where the authorities get the most impact for their enforcement dollars. A cocaine dealer, even a small retail pusher, often supplies dozens or even hundreds of users each day, as did "speakeasies" (illegal saloons) during Prohibition; a hooker typically services anywhere from three to ten tricks a day. By incarcerating the supplier, the police can prevent several—or even several hundred—transactions from taking place, an outcome that is usually much more cost effective than going after the buyers one by one. This is not to say that the police ignore the consumers of illegal goods; indeed, "sting" operations—in which the police pose as illicit sellers—often make the headlines. Nevertheless, most enforcement efforts focus on the supply side, and so too shall we.

Fundamentally, law enforcement activities directed against the suppliers of illegal goods drive up costs of operation for suppliers. Risking fines, jail sentences, and possibly even violence becomes part of the costs of doing business and must be taken into account by existing and potential suppliers. Some entrepreneurs will simply leave the business, turning their talents to other activities; others will resort to clandestine (and costly) means to hide their operations from the police; still others will restrict the circle of buyers with whom they are willing to deal, so as to minimize the chances that a customer is a cop. Across the board, the costs of operation are higher, and *at any given price*, less of the product will be available. There is a reduction in supply, and the result is a higher price for the good.

Now, this increase in price is, in a sense, exactly what the enforcement officials are after, for the consumers of sex, booze, and drugs behave according to the law of demand: The higher the price of a good, the lower the amount consumed. So the immediate impact of the enforcement efforts against sellers is to reduce the consumption of the illegal good by buyers. There are, however, some other effects.

First, since the good in question is now illegal, people who have a comparative advantage in conducting illegal activities will be attracted to the business of supplying (and perhaps demanding) the good. Some may have an existing criminal record and are relatively unconcerned about adding to it. Others have developed skills in evading detection and prosecution while engaged in other criminal activities. Some may simply look at the newly illegal activity as another means of thumbing their nose at society. The general point is that when an activity is made illegal, people who are good at being criminals are attracted to that activity.

Normally, illegal contracts are not enforceable through legal channels.[2] Thus, buyers and sellers of illegal goods frequently must resort to private methods of contract enforcement—which often means violence.[3] As a result, people who are relatively good at violence are attracted to illegal activities, and are given greater incentives to employ their talents. This is one of the reasons why the murder rate in America rose to record levels during Prohibition (1920–1933) and then dropped sharply when intoxicating liquor was again made legal. It also helps explain why the numbers of drug-related murders are currently rising at record rates, and why "drive-by" shootings have become commonplace in many drug-infested cities. The Thompson submachine gun of the 1930s and

[2]And even if they were, few prostitutes, drug dealers, or suppliers of illegal whiskey would be stupid enough to complain to the police about, for example, not being paid for their products.

[3]Fundamentally, violence—such as involuntary incarceration—plays a key role in the government's enforcement of legal contracts. We often do not think of it as violence, of course, because it is usually cushioned by constitutional safeguards, procedural rules, etc.

the MAC-10 machine gun of the 1980s were, importantly, just the low-cost means of contract enforcement.

The attempts of law officers to drive sellers of illegal goods out of business has another effect. At recent wholesale prices, $50,000 worth of cocaine weighs about 4 pounds; $50,000 worth of marijuana weighs about 200 pounds. As any drug smuggler worth her salt can tell you, hiding 4 pounds of contraband is a lot easier than hiding 200 pounds. The same fact is true at all levels of the distribution process. Thus, to avoid detection and prosecution, suppliers of the illegal good have an incentive to direct their efforts toward the more valuable versions of their product—which for drugs and booze means the more potent versions. Bootleggers during Prohibition concentrated on hard liquor rather than beer and wine; even today, "moonshine" typically has roughly twice the alcohol content of legal hard liquor (such as bourbon, scotch, or vodka). After narcotics became illegal in this country in 1914, importers switched from the milder opium to its more valuable, more potent, and more addictive derivative, heroin.

The move to the more potent versions of illegal commodities is enhanced by enforcement activities directed against *users*. Not only do users, like suppliers, find it easier (cheaper) to hide the more potent versions, there is also a change in relative prices due to user penalties. Typically, the law has lower penalties for using an illegal substance than for distributing it. Within each category (use or sale), however, there is commonly the same penalty regardless of value per unit. For example, during Prohibition, a bottle of wine and a bottle of more expensive, more potent hard liquor were equally illegal. Today, the possession of one gram of, say, 90 percent pure cocaine brings the same penalty as the possession of one gram of 10 percent pure cocaine. Given the physical quantities, there is a fixed cost (the legal penalty) associated with being caught, regardless of value per unit (and thus potency) of the substance. Hence, the structure of legal penalties raises the relative price of less potent versions, encouraging users to substitute more potent versions—heroin instead of opium, hashish instead of marijuana, hard liquor instead of beer.

Penalties against users also encourage a change in the *nature* of usage. Prior to 1914, cocaine was legal in this country and was used openly as a mild stimulant, much as people today use caffeine.[4] This type of usage—small, regular doses over long time intervals—becomes relatively more expensive when the substance is made illegal. "Extensive" usage (small doses spread over time) is more likely to be detected by the authorities than is "intensive" usage (a large dose consumed at once), simply because possession time is longer and the drug must be accessed more frequently. Thus, when a substance is made illegal, there is an incentive for consumers to switch toward usage that is more intensive. In the case of cocaine, rather than ingesting it orally in the form of a highly diluted liquid solution, as was commonly done before 1914, people switched to snorting or even injecting it. During Prohibition, people dispensed with cocktails before dinner each night; instead, on the less frequent occasions when they drank, they more often drank to get drunk.[5]

Not surprisingly, the suppliers of illegal commodities are reluctant to advertise their wares openly; the police are every bit as capable of reading billboards and watching TV as are potential customers. Suppliers are also reluctant to establish easily recognized identities and regular places and hours of business, because to do so increases the chances of being caught by the police. In effect, information about price and quality of products being sold goes "underground," often with unfortunate effects for consumers.

---

[4]The fictional detective Sherlock Holmes—portrayed as a regular user of cocaine—was, in this regard, representative of the society in which he lived. Cocaine was even included as an ingredient in the original formulation of Coca-Cola.

[5]The same phenomenon is observed today. People under the age of 21 consume alcoholic beverages less frequently than do people over the age of 21. But when they do drink, they are more likely to drink to get drunk.

With legal goods, consumers have several means of obtaining information. They can find out about products from friends, from advertisements, and from personal experience. When goods are legal, they can be trademarked for identification. The trademark may not legally be copied, and the courts protect it. Given such easily identified brands, consumers can be made aware of the quality and price of each via the recommendations of friends and advertisements. If their experience does not jibe with their anticipations, they can assure themselves of no further encounter with the unsatisfactory product by never buying that brand again.

When a general class of products becomes illegal, there are fewer ways of obtaining information. Brand names are no longer protected by law, so falsification of well-known ones ensues. When products do not meet expectations, it is more difficult (costly) for consumers to punish suppliers. Frequently, the result of these forces is degradation of product quality and a rise in uncertainty about the nature of that quality. The consequences for consumers of the illegal goods are often unpleasant, sometimes fatal.

Consider prostitution. In those counties in Nevada where prostitution is legal, the ladies of pleasure are required to register with the local authorities, and they generally conduct their business within the confines of well-established bordellos. These establishments, such as the Mustang Ranch and Sally's Ranch, advertise openly and rely heavily on repeat business. Health officials test the prostitutes weekly for venereal disease and monthly for AIDS. Contrast this with other areas of the country, where prostitution is illegal. Suppliers generally are streetwalkers, because a fixed, physical location is too easy for the police to detect and raid. Suppliers change locations frequently, to reduce harassment by police. Repeat business is reported to be minimal; frequently, customers have never seen the prostitute before and will never see her again.

The difference in outcomes is striking. In Nevada, the spread of VD by legal prostitutes is estimated to be "almost nonexistent"; and to date, *none* of the 9000 registered prostitutes in Nevada has tested positive for AIDS. By contrast, in some major cities outside of Nevada the incidence of venereal disease among prostitutes is estimated to be near 100 percent. In Miami, one study found that 19 percent of all incarcerated prostitutes tested positive for AIDS; in Newark, N.J., 52 percent of the prostitutes tested were infected with the AIDS virus. Because of the lack of reliable information in markets for illegal goods, customers frequently don't know exactly what they are getting; as a consequence, they sometimes get more than they bargained for.

Consider alcohol and drugs. Today, alcoholic beverages are heavily advertised to establish their brand names, and are carried by reputable dealers. Customers can readily punish suppliers for any deviation from the expected potency or quality—by withdrawing their business, telling their friends, or even by bringing a lawsuit. Similar circumstances prevailed before 1914 in this country for many products containing opium and cocaine.

During Prohibition, consumers of alcohol often did not know exactly what they were buying or where to find the supplier the next day if they were dissatisfied. Fly-by-night operators sometimes adulterated liquor with *methyl* alcohol. In extremely small concentrations, the result was to make watered-down booze taste like it had more "kick"; in only slightly higher concentrations, the methyl alcohol blinded or even killed the unsuspecting consumer. Even in "reputable" speakeasies (those likely to be in business at the same location the next day), bottles bearing the labels of high-priced foreign whiskeys were refilled repeated with locally (and illegally) produced "rotgut" until, ultimately, their labels wore off.

In the 1970s, more than one purchaser of what was reputed to be high-potency Panama Red or Acapulco Gold marijuana ended up with low-potency pot heavily loaded with stems, seeds, and maybe even oregano. In the 1980s, buyers of cocaine had to worry about not only how much the product had been "cut" along the distribution chain, but also what had been used to cut it. Thus, in recent years the purity of cocaine at the retail level has ranged between 10 percent and 95 percent; for heroin, the degree of purity has ranged from 5 percent to 40 percent. Cutting agents can turn out to be any of various sugars, local anesthetics, or amphetamines; on occasion, rat poison has been used.

We noted earlier that the legal penalties for the users of illegal goods encouraged them to use more potent forms and to use them more intensively. These facts and the uncertain quality and potency of the illegal products make for a deadly combination. During Prohibition, the death rate from acute alcohol poisoning (i.e., due to an overdose) was more than *30 times* higher than it is today. During 1927 alone, 12,000 people died from acute alcohol poisoning, and many thousands more were blinded or killed by contaminated booze. Today, about 3000 people per year die as a direct result of consuming either cocaine or heroin. Of that total, it is estimated, roughly 80 percent die from (1) an overdose caused by unexpectedly potent product, or (2) an adverse reaction to the material used to cut the drug. Clearly, *caveat emptor* (let the buyer beware) is a warning to be taken seriously if one is consuming an illegal product.

We also mentioned at the outset that one of the effects of making a good illegal is to raise its price. One might well ask, by how much? During the late 1980s, the federal government was spending almost $2 billion a year in its efforts to stop the importation of cocaine from Colombia. One recent study of these efforts concluded that these efforts had hiked the price of cocaine by 4 percent (yes, 4 percent) relative to what it would have been had the federal government done nothing to interdict cocaine imports. To hike the price of cocaine an additional 2 percent, the study estimated, would cost the government an extra $1 billion per year in interdiction expenditures.[6]

---

[6]Federal attempts to prevent cocaine from entering the country are, of course, supplemented by other federal, as well as state and local, efforts to eradicate the drug once it has crossed our borders. To date, there are no empirical estimates of the extent to which these other efforts have increased prices.

It is believed that the government's efforts to halt imports of marijuana have been somewhat more successful, presumably because that product is easier to detect than cocaine. Nevertheless, suppliers have responded by cultivating marijuana domestically, instead of importing it. The net effect has been even greater total supplies, accompanied by an estimated *10-fold* increase in potency, due to the superior farming techniques available in this country.[7]

We might also consider the government's efforts to eliminate the consumption of alcohol during the 1920s and 1930s. They failed so badly that the Eighteenth Amendment—which put Prohibition in place—was the first (and thus far the only) Constitutional amendment ever to be repealed. As for prostitution, well, it is reputed to be "the oldest profession," and by all accounts continues flourishing today, even in Newark and Miami.

The government's inability to halt the consumption of sex, booze, or drugs does not, of itself, mean that those efforts have simply failed. Indeed, the "successes" of these efforts are manifested in their consequences—ranging from tainted drugs and alcohol to disease-ridden prostitutes. The message instead is that when the government attempts to prevent mutually beneficial exchange, even its best efforts are unlikely to meet with spectacular success.

DISCUSSION QUESTIONS

1. The federal government currently taxes alcohol on the basis of the "100 proof gallon." (One hundred proof alcohol is exactly 50 percent pure ethyl alcohol; most hard liquor is 80 proof, i.e., 40 percent ethyl alcohol, whereas wine is usually about 24 proof and most beer is 6–10 proof.) How would alcohol consumption pat-

---

[7]There are even reliable reports that some growers in the U.S. are now using genetic bio-engineering to improve their strains. In effect, the government's (partially) successful efforts to stop the importation of marijuana inadvertently have resulted in technological improvements in marijuana cultivation.

terns be different if the government taxed alcohol strictly on the basis of volume, rather than taking into account its potency as well?

2. During Prohibition, some speakeasy operators paid bribes to ensure that the police did not raid them. Would you expect the quality of the liquor served in such speakeasies to be higher or lower than in speakeasies that did not pay such bribes? Would you expect any systematic differences (e.g., with regard to income levels) of the customers patronizing the two types of speakeasies?

2

Pity the Poor Farmer— All the Way to the Bank

Bruce Hoskens has a problem—finding oats. Now, oats may not sound like a big deal, but Hoskens is an executive for the Quaker Oats Co.—and Quaker Oats is running out of oats. The steep decline in U.S. oats production during the late '80s "strikes terror in our hearts," says a buyer for Quaker, and the General Mills cereal company isn't any happier. Recent U.S. oat harvests have been the lowest in more than a century, forcing General Mills to bring in oats from Argentina. Quaker, in its bid to find supplies of high-quality U.S. oats, has been serenading midwestern farmers with 60-second radio spots promising "high bids for top-quality grain." It has even tried enlisting farm youths in oats-growing contests, with ads declaring, "Quaker Oats Co. is looking for you!"

If all of this sounds a bit peculiar for a nation that prides itself as the bread basket of the world, your instincts are on the mark. After all, American farms are so productive that we have taken 78 million acres—122,000 square *miles*—out of production to curb grain surpluses. At first blush, the droughts of the late 1980s might seem like a plausible explanation for the missing oats. Yet the decline in oats production began two years before the rains stopped, and in any event, most prime oats acreage was unscathed by the dry weather. Solving this mystery will instead require a trip back in time—nearly 100 years.

The two decades before World War I witnessed unparalleled agricultural prosperity in the United States. This "golden age of American farming" continued through the war, as food prices soared. The end of the war, combined with a sharp depression in 1920, brought the golden age to a painful halt. Even the eight years of economic recovery from 1921 to 1929—the Roaring Twenties—did little to help American farmers. European countries were redirecting their resources into agricultural production, and new American tariffs on foreign goods severely disrupted international trade. Since food exports had been an important source of farmers' incomes, the decline in world trade reduced the demand for American agricultural products and cut deeply into food prices and farm incomes.

The sharply falling food prices of the 1920s led farmers to view their problem as one of relative overproduction. Numerous cooperative efforts were made to restrict production, but virtually all of them failed. Most crops were produced under highly competitive conditions, with large numbers of buyers and sellers dealing in products that were largely undifferentiated: One farmer's corn, for example, was the same as any other farmer's corn. Thus, producers were unable to enforce collective output restrictions and price hikes on a voluntary basis. But what farmers failed to do by voluntary means in the 1920s, they accomplished via government directives in the 1930s. An effective farm **price-support** program was instituted in 1933, marking the beginning of a policy of farm subsidies in the United States that continues even today.

We can best understand the results of price supports and other government farm programs by first examining the market for agricultural commodities in the absence of government intervention. In that competitive market, a large number of farmers supply amounts of each commodity, such as corn. The sum of the quantities that indivdual farmers supply at various prices makes up the **market supply** schedule of a commodity. Each farmer supplies only a small part of the market total. This cannot influence the price of the product. If the farmer were to raise the price, anyone wishing to purchase corn could easily buy from someone else at the **market-clearing, or equilibrium, price**. And no farmers would sell below the market-clearing price, since they can sell all they produce at the market-clearing price. Thus, every unit of output sold by farmers goes for the same price. The price received for the last (or *marginal*) unit sold is exactly the same as that received for all the rest.

The farmer will produce corn up to the point that, if one more unit were produced, its production cost would be greater than the price received. Notice that at higher prices, farmers can incur higher costs for additional units produced and still make a **profit**. Since all farmers face the same basic production decision, all farmers together will produce more at higher prices. Indeed, no farmer will stop producing until he stops making a profit on additional units. That is, each farmer will end up selling corn at the market-clearing price, which will equal his costs of production plus a normal profit.[1]

Now, how has the usual price-support program worked? The government has decided what constitutes a "fair price." The key to this vital determination is the ratio between the prices farmers historically paid for what they bought and the prices they received during "good" years—such as during agriculture's golden age. Except for the years of World War II,

---

[1]For society as a whole, this is actually a cost of production, since it is required to keep the farmer growing corn instead of changing to an alternative occupation.

the "fair" price decreed by the government (called the **parity** price) generally has been well above the market equilibrium price that would have prevailed in the absence of price supports. This has encouraged farmers to produce more, and induced consumers to consume less. Thus, there typically have been large **surpluses** for most crops covered by price supports.

How has the government made the parity price "stick" in the face of these surpluses? It has agreed to buy the crops, such as corn, at their parity price.[2] (As a practical matter, these purchases have been disguised as "loans" from a government agency called the Commodity Credit Corporation (CCC)— loans that never need be repaid.) Historically, the government has either stored the crops it purchases, sold them on the world market (as opposed to the domestic market) at prices well below the U.S. support price, or simply given them away to foreign nations under the "Food for Peace" program. In each instance, the result has been substantial costs for taxpayers—and substantial gains for farmers. In *each* of several recent years, for example, American taxpayers have forked over better than $10 *billion* for the benefit of corn farmers alone. Smaller, but still quite substantial, subsidies are garnered by the producers of wheat, peanuts, soybeans, sorghum, rice, and cotton—to name but a few.

In an effort to keep the size of the surpluses down, the government has restricted the number of acres that farmers may cultivate. Under these various **acreage restriction programs**, farmers wishing to participate in government subsidy programs must agree to keep a certain amount of land out of production. Currently about 78 million acres—an area the size of New Mexico—are covered by the agreements. Enticed by high support prices, farmers have been ingenious in finding ways to evade acreage restrictions. For example, soybeans and

---

[2]Actually, the support price at which the government has purchased crops typically has been somewhat below the level that would give farmers complete parity.

sorghum are both excellent substitutes for corn as a source of livestock feed. So farmers agreed to cut their corn acreage, and then planted soybeans or sorghum on the land. This aggravated the corn surplus, and forced the government to extend acreage restrictions and price supports to soybeans and sorghum. Similarly, faced with limitations on the amount of land they can cultivate, farmers have responded by cultivating what remains far more *intensively*. They have used more fertilizer and pesticides, introduced more sophisticated methods of planting and irrigation, and applied technological advances in farm machinery at every opportunity. As a result, agricultural output per man-hour is now *10 times* what it was 60 years ago.

The effects of price supports and acreage restrictions, combined with farmers' efforts to evade these restrictions, thus have been threefold. First, consumers have paid more—about $5 billion per year more—for those products whose support prices exceed the prices that otherwise would prevail. Second, more taxpayers' money—about $20 billion per year more—is expended on agriculture than otherwise would be spent. And third, surpluses of crops have continued to pile up in government silos and warehouses. By the late 1980s, according to one observer, the CCC had enough wheat in its storage bins to make seven loaves of bread for every man, woman, and child in the *world*. There are currently 5 billion surplus bushels of corn in CCC granaries and mountains of soybeans, beet sugar, and other farm products in buildings, caves, and other storage facilities owned or leased by the CCC.

Beginning about 15 years ago, the government tried to cut back on surpluses—and add to farmers' incomes—by encouraging exports. To accomplish this, however, support prices for farm products had to be lowered to a level where they would be competitive on world markets. To compensate farmers for the lower support prices, "target prices" for agricultural products were established. If the market price for, say, wheat fell below the target price, then the government would pay the difference in cash to the farmer. The target-price system helped cut surpluses, but ran into two problems.

First, the government overlooked the fact that the world market for agriculture was changing, and that U.S. exports were no longer essential to many foreign countries. India and China were expanding production to the point that they could fully supply their domestic markets. Brazil was doubling the amount of land under cultivation, ultimately making it a net exporter of agricultural products. Even Saudi Arabia developed agricultural surpluses—storing them in idle oil tankers. The "green revolution" in the Third World—made possible, ironically, by U.S. foreign aid—was transforming the global market for food products. As a result, U.S. food exports failed to meet expectations; indeed, by the mid-1980s America was actually importing more food than it was exporting.

The second problem with the target-price system was that it made farm subsidies painfully clear to the taxpayers who were footing the bill. Price supports hide subsidies by making it appear as though the resulting crop surpluses are the result of American farmers simply being "too productive" for their own good. With the direct cash payments made under the target-price system, however, it became apparent that the government was taking money out of taxpayers' pockets with one hand and giving it to farmers with the other hand. Moreover, the target-price system, like our other agricultural programs, geared the size of the subsidies to the amount of output produced by the recipients. Thus, small farmers received trivial amounts, while giant farms—agribusinesses—collected giant subsidies. The owners of many huge cotton farms and rice farms, for example, received payments totaling more than $1 million apiece.

Faced with the prospect of a taxpayer revolt, Congress tried to fix things up with the Farm Security Act of 1985—and once again missed the mark. This legislation initially replaced cash payments to farmers with a "payment-in-kind" (PIK) program. Instead of writing checks to farmers, the PIK scheme authorized the U.S. Deparment of Agriculture to give farmers surplus commodities held in storage by the CCC. Farmers could use the commodities as livestock feed or simply sell them at the going market price. The PIK program helped cut surpluses and encourage exports initially, but only at great cost— roughly $30 billion a year. Moreover, the law locked many farmers into growing the same crop year after year, regardless of market conditions. If farmers don't plant a specified percentage of their "crop base" each year, their subsidy payments are subsequently reduced. The result has been huge crop surpluses in the lucrative corn and wheat programs.

The Farm Security Act also tinkered with support prices for many crops—which brings us back to oats. The law created a 96-cents-a-bushel differential in subsidies for barley over oats. Not surprisingly, farmers in droves abandoned oats—just as consumer demand for oatmeal and other oat-based products was picking up. The farmers are happy growing barley, but cereal producers are, well, oatless. Indeed, when asked what he thought about current U.S. farm policy, the chief of procurement for General Mills remarked, "That's the silliest thing I've ever heard of." Can you blame him?

DISCUSSION QUESTIONS

1. Can you explain why the government goes to such lengths to increase the incomes of farmers? Is your explanation consistent with the observation that a large portion of government subsidies benefits giant agribusinesses?
2. Why do you think the government spends millions of dollars each year storing crop surpluses, instead of just burning the surpluses or selling them back to farmers to use as fertilizer for next year's crop?

3

Raising the
Minimum Wage

Ask workers if they would like a raise, and the answer is likely
to be a resounding yes. But ask them if they would like to be
fired or have their hours of work reduced, and they would
probably tell you no. The fight over the **minimum wage** is focused on exactly these points.

Proponents of the minimum wage—the lowest hourly
wage firms may legally pay their workers—argue that low-
income workers are underpaid and unable to support themselves or their families. The minimum wage, they say, hikes
earnings at the bottom end of the wage distribution, with little
or no disruption to workers or businesses. Opponents claim
that most potential low-wage workers are low-skilled youths
without families to support. The minimum wage, it is said,
merely enriches a few teenagers at the far greater expense of
many others, who lose their jobs. Most important, opponents

argue, most low-wage workers lack the skills needed for employers to hire them at the current federal minimum wage. Unable to get work, these individuals (mostly teenagers) never learn the basic on-the-job skills needed to move up the economic ladder to higher-paying employment. The battle lines are clearly drawn—but what are the facts?

The federal minimum wage was instituted in 1938 as a provision of the Fair Labor Standards Act (FLSA). It was originally set at $0.25 an hour, about 40 percent of the average manufacturing wage at the time. Over the next 40 years, the legal minimum was raised periodically, roughly in accord with the movement of market wages throughout the economy. Typically, its level has averaged between 40 percent and 50 percent of average manufacturing wages. In response to the high inflation of the late 1970s, the minimum wage was hiked seven times between 1974 and 1981, reaching $3.35 an hour—about 42 percent of manufacturing wages. Ronald Reagan vowed to keep a lid on the minimum wage, and by the time he stepped down as president, the minimum's unchanged level left it at 31 percent of average wages. In 1989, after vetoing a hike in the minimum wage to $4.55 per hour, President Bush signed legislation that raised the minimum to $3.80 per hour in 1990 and $4.25 in 1991.[1]

Supporters of the minimum wage—currently paid to nearly 5 million workers, about 9 percent of the hourly wage earners in the United States—argue that it prevents exploitation of employees and helps them earn enough to support their families and themselves. Even so, a full-time minimum-wage worker earns less than $9000 a year, which is less than what the government considers enough to keep a family of three out of poverty, and only 75 percent of what's needed for a family of four. It is figures like these that keep the impetus behind efforts to raise the minimum wage; even at, say, $5.00

---

[1]The legislation also provided for a "training" wage (equal to 85 percent of the minimum wage) for inexperienced teenagers during their first ninety days on the job.

an hour, a family of four with one wage earner would still be under the poverty line.

Yet those who oppose the minimum wage note that two-thirds of those workers earning the minimum wage are single, and they earn enough to put them 30 percent *above* the poverty cutoff. Moreover, about half of these single workers are teenagers, most of whom have no financial obligations, except possibly for clothing and car insurance expenditures. Raising the minimum, opponents say, chiefly benefits upper-middle-class teens, who are least in need of assistance, at the same time that it costs the jobs of thousands of disadvantaged minority youths.

Only a few commentators dispute the fact that the higher minimum wage will cost some current or prospective workers their jobs. After all, the number of workers demanded, like the quantity demanded for all goods, responds to price: The higher the price, the lower the number desired. Yet there *is* debate over *how many* jobs will be lost due to raising the minimum wage from $3.35 an hour to $4.25. The lowest credible estimates put the number at 50,000; the highest estimates gauge the job loss at roughly 400,000. With a work force of 125 million persons, this may not sound like very many people. But most of the people who will be fired, or at least not hired, will be teenagers, about 6 million of whom now have jobs. The *average* estimate of jobs lost due to raising the minimum wage to $4.25 an hour runs about 250,000—which means that roughly 1 of 25 teens now working will lose their job.

Significantly, the youths most likely to lose work as a result of the higher minimum wage are disadvantaged teenagers, primarily minorities. On average, these teens enter the work force with the fewest job skills and the greatest need for on-the-job training. Until and unless these disadvantaged teenagers are allowed to acquire these skills, they are the most likely to suffer job losses due to the higher minimum wage—and thus the least likely to have the opportunity to move up the economic ladder. With a teen unemployment rate better than triple the overall rate, and unemployment among black youngsters hovering above 30 percent, critics of the minimum wage argue that the higher minimum is one of the worst things that could befall this group.

Indeed, the minimum wage has an aspect that not many of its supporters are inclined to discuss: It can make employers more likely to discriminate on the basis of sex or race. When wages are determined by market forces, employers who would discriminate on the basis of sex or race face a reduced, and thus more expensive, pool of workers. But when the government mandates an above-market wage, a surplus of low-skill workers results, and it becomes easier and cheaper to discriminate. As Professor Lawrence Summers of Harvard University notes, the minimum wage "removes the economic penalty to the employer. He can choose the one who's white with blond hair."

Critics of the minimum wage also argue that the higher minimum will make firms less willing to train workers lacking basic skills. Instead, companies may choose to hire only experienced workers whose abilities justify the higher wage. Firms are also likely to become less generous with fringe benefits in an effort to hold down labor costs. The prospect of more discrimination, less job training for low-skill workers, and fewer fringe benefits for entry-level workers leaves many observers uncomfortable. As economist Jacob Mincer of Columbia University notes, raising the minimum wage means "a loss of opportunity" for the hard-core unemployed.

When Congress and the President agreed in 1989 to raise the minimum wage, it was only after a heated battle lasting ten months. Given the stakes involved, it is not surprising that discussions of the minimum wage soon turn to controversy. As one former high-level U.S. Department of Labor official has said: "When it comes to the minimum wage, there are no easy positions to take. Either you are in favor of more jobs, less discrimination, and more on-the-job training, or you support better wages for workers. Whatever stance you choose, you are bound to get clobbered by the opposition." And whenever

Congress and the President face this issue, one or both parties usually feels the same way.

DISCUSSION QUESTIONS

1. Are teenagers better off when a higher minimum wage enables some to get higher wages but causes others to lose their jobs?
2. Are there methods other than a higher minimum wage that could raise the incomes of low-wage workers without interfering with the operation of the labor market?

4

Water, Water Everywhere, Nor Any Drop to Drink?

Mono Lake is dying. Over the past 50 years, this California lake—our country's oldest lake, and one of its most beautiful—has shrunk from more than 80 square miles in area to about 60. Why? Because since 1941, most of the eastern Sierra mountain water that once fed Mono Lake has been disappearing down a 225-mile-long aquaduct, south to Los Angeles, where it is used to wash cars, sprinkle lawns, and otherwise lubricate the life-style of southern California. Environmentalists cry out that the diversion of water from Mono Lake must stop. Los Angelenos, who pay $230 per acre-foot for the water, claim there are no viable alternative sources. Central California farmers, who pay but $10 per acre-foot for subsidized water from the *western* side of the Sierras, fear that diverting their own "liquid gold" to save Mono Lake would dry up their livelihood. Meanwhile, this migratory rest stop for hundreds of thousands of birds is disappearing.

The issues that have arisen over the future of Mono Lake are surfacing in hundreds of locations throughout the United States. Conservationists are increasingly concerned about the toxic contamination of our water supply and the depletion of our underground water sources. Extensive irrigation projects in the western states use more than 150 *billion* gallons of water a day—seven times as much water as all the nation's city water systems combined. The Ogallala aquifer (a 20-million-acre lake beneath the beef-and-bread-basket states of Colorado, Kansas, Nebraska, New Mexico, Oklahoma, and Texas) is currently dropping by three feet a year—because 150,000 wells are pumping water out faster than nature can replenish it.

The common view of water is that it is an overused, precious **resource**, and that we are running out of it. The economic analysis of the water "problem," however, is not quite so pessimistic, nor so tied to the physical quantities of water that exist on our earth and in the atmosphere. Rather, an economic analysis of water follows along lines similar to an analysis of any other scarce resources.

The water industry is one of the oldest and largest in the United States, and the philosophy surrounding it merits some analysis. Many commentators believe that water is unique, that it should not be treated as an **economic good**, that is, a scarce good. Engineering studies that concern themselves with demand for residential water typically use a "requirements" approach. The forecaster simply predicts population changes and then multiplies those estimates by currently available data showing the average amount of water used per person. The underlying assumption for such a forecast is that, *regardless of the price charged* for water in the future, the same quantity will be demanded. Implicitly, then, both the short- and long-run price elasticities of demand are assumed to be zero.

But is this really the case? Perhaps not. Consider, for example, the cities of Tucson and Phoenix, Arizona. Although these cities are located only 100 miles apart, their water-usage rates are notably different. While the average household in Phoenix uses 260 gallons per day, in Tucson the average usage is only 160 gallons per day. Could this usage differential be accounted for by the fact that water costs only about half as much per gallon in Phoenix as it does in Tucson? Before we jump to such a conclusion, let's look at a study of water prices in Boulder, Colorado, conducted by economist Steve Hanke.

Boulder was selected by Hanke because in 1961 the water utility in Boulder installed water meters in every home and business that it supplied. Prior to 1961, Boulder, like many other municipalities in the United States, had charged a flat monthly rate for water. Each household paid a specified amount of dollars per month no matter how much (or little) water was used. In essence, the flat fee charged prior to 1961 meant that a zero price was being charged at the margin (for any incremental use of water). The introduction of usage meters meant that a positive price for the marginal unit of water was now imposed.

Hanke looked at the quantity of water demanded both before and after the meters were installed in Boulder.[1] He first developed what he calls the "ideal" use of water for each month throughout the year. He completed his "ideal" use estimates by taking account of the average irrigable area per residence, the average temperature during the month, the average number of daylight hours, and the effect of rainfall. The term *ideal* implies nothing from an economic point of view, merely indicating the minimum quantity of sprinkling water required to maintain the aesthetic quality of each residence's lawn.

From the data in Table 4-1, which compares water usage in Boulder with and without metering, we find that individuals sprinkled their lawns much more under the flat-rate system than they did under the metered-rate system. Column 1

[1]"Demand for Water under Dynamic Conditions," *Water Resources Research*, vol. 6, no. 5 (October 1970), pp. 1253–1261.

TABLE 4-1   Comparing Water Usage With and Without Metering of Actual Usage

(1) Meter Routes	(2) Actual Sprinkling to Ideal Sprinkling, Flat- Rate Period	(3) Actual Sprinkling to Ideal Sprinkling, Metered-Rate Period
16, 18	128	78
37	175	72
53, 54	156	72
70, 71, 72	177	63
73, 75	175	97
74	175	102
76, 78	176	105
79	157	86

Source: Steve Hanke, "Demand for Water Under Dynamic Conditions," *Water Resources Research*, vol. 6, no. 5 (October 1970).

of the table shows the meter route numbers arbitrarily assigned by the municipality. Column 2 shows how much water was used in the different routes during the period when a flat rate was charged for water usage. It is expressed in terms of actual sprinkling compared to "ideal" sprinkling. The data presented in column 3 are for the one-year period after the metering system was put into effect. Actual sprinkling is compared to "ideal" sprinkling, but under a system of metered-rate pricing in which each user is charged for the actual amount of water used. Since less water is used in the presence of metering (which raises the price of incremental water), Hanke's data indicate that the quantity of water demanded is a function of the price charged for water. Moreover, Hanke found that for many years after the imposition of the metered-rate pricing system for water, the quantity of water demanded not only remained at a lower level than before metering, but continued to fall slightly. That, of course, means that the long-run price elasticity of demand for water was greater than the short-run price elasticity of demand.

Would attaching a dollar sign to water help to solve problems of recurring water **shortages** and endemic waste? Many economists feel it would. It is well known, for example, that much of the water supplied by federal irrigation projects is wasted by farmers and other users because they have no incentive to conserve water and curb overconsumption. The federal government, which has subsidized water projects since 1902, allots water to certain districts, communities, or farmers on the basis of previous usage "requirements." That means that if farmers in a certain irrigation district were to conserve on water usage by, say, upgrading their irrigation systems, their water allotment would eventually be reduced. As a result, a "use it or lose it" attitude has prevailed among users of federal water. Water supplied by federal water projects is also cheap. The Congressional Budget Office has estimated that users pay only about 19 percent of the total cost of the water they get.

Economists have suggested that raising the price of federal water would lead to more efficient and less wasteful water consumption. A study by B. Delworth Gardner, an economist at the University of California at Davis, for example, concludes that a 10 percent rise in prices could reduce water use on some California farm crops by as much as 20 percent. Support for such a price rise is politically difficult, however, because federal law stipulates that ability to pay, as well as cost, must be considered when determining water prices.

An alternative solution has been proposed by some economists, involving the trading and sale of water rights held by existing federal water users. Such a solution, it is felt, would benefit the economy overall because it could help curb water waste, prevent water shortages, and lessen the need for costly new water projects. To some extent, trading and sales of water rights have already taken place—for example, in California and Utah, and environmentalists are currently trying to arrange market exchanges of water rights to help save Mono Lake. Numerous federal and state laws have, to date, made such trading very difficult.

Until recent years, it had been thought that there was so much water we simply did not have to worry about it—there was always another river or another well to draw on if we ran short. Putting a price tag on water would require a substantial change in the way we have traditionally thought about water. Is this possible or even desirable? If it is not, one fact seems certain: The birds of Mono Lake soon will have to look elsewhere for their water.

DISCUSSION QUESTIONS

1. In your opinion, do the data presented in Table 6-1 refute the "water is different" philosophy?
2. How much water does your neighbor "need?" Is your answer the same if *you* have to pay your neighbor's water bill?

5

Flying the Friendly Skies?

Just about everybody hops into their cars with little thought for their personal safety, beyond, perhaps, the act of putting on seat belts. Yet even though travel on scheduled, commercial airlines is *100 times* safer than driving to work or to the grocery store, many people approach air travel with a sense of foreboding, if not downright fear.

If we were to systematically organize our thoughts on the wisdom of traveling 600 miles an hour in an aluminum tube seven miles above the earth, several questions might come to mind: How safe *is* this? How safe *should* it be? Since the people who operate airlines are not in it for fun, does their interest in making a buck ignore my interest in making it home in one piece? Since **competition** among the airlines has heated up to unprecedented levels (on many routes, the engines don't even cool off before the planes have headed for another takeoff), are competitive pressures forcing the airlines to skimp on passenger safety?

The science of economics begins with one simple principle: We live in a world of scarcity. As a result, to get more of any good, we must sacrifice some of other goods. This is just as true of safety as it is of pizzas or haircuts or works of art. Safety confers benefits (we live longer and more enjoyably), but achieving it also entails costs (we must give up something to obtain that safety).

As the degree of safety rises, the *total* benefits of safety rise but the *marginal* (or incremental) benefits of *additional* safety decline. Consider a simple example: Having four exit doors on an airplane instead of three increases the number of people who can safely escape in the event of an emergency evacuation. Analogously, having five doors rather than four would enable more people to evacuate safely. In both cases, more doors mean more people evacuated without injury, so the total benefits from safety rise with the number of doors. Nevertheless, the *fifth* door adds less in safety benefits (in terms of injuries avoided or lives saved) than does the *fourth* door; if the fourth enables, say, an extra ten people to escape, the fifth may enable only an extra six to escape.[1] So we say that the *marginal* (or incremental) benefit of safety declines as the amount of safety increases.

Let's look now at the other side of the equation: As the amount of safety increases, both the total and the marginal (or incremental) *costs* of providing safety *rise*. Having a fuel gauge on the plane's instrument panel clearly enhances safety, since it reduces the chance that the plane will run out of fuel while in

---

[1]If this sounds implausible, imagine having a door for each person; the last door added will enable at most one more person to escape.

flight.[2] It is always possible that a fuel gauge will malfunction, so having a *backup* fuel gauge also adds to safety. Since having two gauges is more costly than having just one, the total costs of safety rise as safety rises. It is also clear, however, that while the cost of the second gauge is (at least) as great as the cost of the first, the second gauge has a smaller positive impact on safety. Thus, the cost per unit of *additional* (or incremental) safety is higher for the second fuel gauge than for the first.

How much safety should we have? For an economist, the answer to such a question is generally expressed in terms of marginal benefits and marginal costs. The economically *efficient* level of safety occurs when the marginal costs of any *more* safety would just exceed the marginal benefits of that extra safety. Consider the example of doors on an airplane. Suppose that having a fourth door confers $1 million in benefits while the costs of adding the door amount to only $300,000. Then the net benefit of having the door is $700,000, and, from an economic standpoint, it is efficient to have the fourth door. Contrast this with the prospect of having 13 doors on an airplane. Suppose that the 13th door confers benefits of $150,000 but that the costs of adding the 13th door are $900,000. In this case, the additional benefits of the door are *less* than the additional costs; adding the door costs more than it is worth, so the door should not be added.

In general, the efficient level of safety will *not* be perfect safety, because perfection is simply too costly to achieve. For example, to be absolutely *certain* that no one was ever killed or injured in an airplane crash, we would have to prevent all travel in airplanes. This does not mean that it is efficient to have airplanes dropping out of the sky like autumn leaves. It

---

[2]Notice that we say "reduces" rather than "eliminates." In 1978 a United Airlines pilot preoccupied with a malfunctioning landing gear evidently failed to pay sufficient attention to his cockpit gauges. Eight people were killed when the plane was forced to crash land after running out of fuel.

does mean that it is efficient for there to be some risk associated with air travel. The unavoidable conclusion is that if we wish to enjoy the advantages of flying, we must be willing to accept some risk—a conclusion that each of us implicitly accepts every time we step aboard an airplane.[3]

Changes in circumstances can alter the efficient level of safety. For example, if a technological change reduces the costs of manufacturing and installing airplane doors, the marginal costs of providing a safe means of exit will be lower. Hence, it will be efficient to have more doors installed, implying that air travel will become safer. Similarly, if the marginal benefits of safety rise for some reason—perhaps because the President of the United States is on board—it will be efficient to take more precautions, resulting in safer air travel. Given the factors that determine the benefits and costs of safety, however, the result will be some determinate level of safety, one that generally will be associated with *some* risk of death or injury.

Do airlines in fact provide the efficient level of safety? If information were free, the answer to this question presumably would have to be yes. Consumers would simply observe the levels of safety provided by different airlines, the prices they

---

[3]The same principles apply to manned space flight, such as the operation of the space shuttle. The National Aeronautics and Space Administration (NASA) recognizes this, and goes so far as to calculate the probabilities that individual components on the space shuttle will fail. For particularly important components, NASA requires that the systems perform with "five-nines reliability," i.e., operate properly 99.999 percent of the time. For less important components, NASA demands only four-nines reliability or even three-nines. Given the many components on the space shuttle (and their interactions), it is possible (although not easy) to calculate the resulting probability of "mission failure"—NASA's euphemism for catastrophic loss of the shuttle and its crew. After the space shuttle *Challenger* disaster in January of 1986, NASA retrospectively calculated the probability of mission failure for the shuttle as 4 percent, i.e., 1 in 25. As it turned out—coincidentally, one must presume—the ill-fated *Challenger* mission was the 25th flight of the shuttle program. Design modifications in the space shuttles have since reduced the probability of mission failure to 2 percent.

charge, and select the degrees of safety that best suited their preferences and budgets—just as with other goods. But, of course, information is not free; it is a scarce good, costly to obtain. As a result, it is possible that passengers are unaware of the safety records of various airlines, just as they may be unaware of the competency of pilots and the maintenance procedures of an airline's mechanics. The fact that information about safety is not free has been used to argue that it is appropriate for the federal government to mandate certain minimum levels of safety, as in fact it does today through the operation of the Federal Aviation Administration (FAA).

Fundamentally, the argument in favor of government safety standards rests on the presumption that, left to their own devices, airlines would provide less safety than passengers actually want to have. This might happen, for example, if customers could not tell (at a reasonable cost) whether or not the equipment, training, procedures, and so on employed by an airline were safe. How many airline passengers are experts in metal fatigue, for example, or are knowledgeable about the amount of training required to pilot a 747 with any specific degree of safety? If passengers cannot cheaply gauge the level of safety, then they will not be willing to reward airlines for being safe, nor punish them for being unsafe. Consider a simple analogy: How much would you pay for a beautiful new set of clothes if the clothes were invisible? Not much, we would guess, unless you happened to be an egotistical emperor. Hence, the reasoning goes, safety is costly to provide, consumers are unwilling to pay for it because they cannot accurately measure it, and so airlines provide too little of it. The conclusion, at least as reached by some, is that we should have a body of government experts—such as the FAA—set safety standards for the industry.

As plausible as this conclusion seems, it ignores two simple points. First, how is the government to know what the efficient level of safety is? Assume for the moment that the FAA employs persons who are experts in metal fatigue, pilot training, maintenance procedures, and so on. Assume also that the FAA knows with great precision both (1) the impact of these matters on the likelihood of deaths and injuries due to plane crashes, and (2) exactly how much it costs to implement various safety improvements.[4] The FAA *still* does not have enough information to set efficient safety standards—because it does not know the value that people place on safety. Without such information, the FAA has no way of assessing the benefits of additional safety, and thus no means of knowing whether those benefits are greater or less than the costs.[5]

The second point is perhaps more fundamental. It is arguable that people are ultimately interested in whether they reach their destinations safely, and not whether they got there because of a good plane, a good pilot, or a good mechanic. Even if they cannot observe whether an airline hires good pilots or bad pilots, they can observe whether that airline's planes land safely or crash—if for no other reason than because airplane crashes are the subject of intense media scrutiny. If it is safety that is important to consumers—and not the obscure, costly-to-measure set of *reasons* for that safety—the fact that consumers cannot easily measure metal fatigue in jet engines may be totally irrelevant to the process of achieving the efficient level of safety. If you know that an airline's planes have a nasty habit of hitting mountains, do you really care whether it is because their pilots have bad eyesight or because their planes have no altimeters?

Interestingly, recent evidence shows that consumers *are* cognizant of the safety performance of airlines, and that they "punish" airlines that perform in an unsafe manner. Researchers have found that when an airline is "at fault" in a fatal plane crash, consumers appear to downgrade their safety rating of the airline (i.e., revise upward their estimates of the

---

[4]Many people would argue that these assumptions presume that the FAA knows more than it could possibly know; we make the assumptions only to present the case for government safety regulations in the best light.

[5]Even if FAA experts know how much *they* benefit from additional safety, how are they to know how much *you* benefit?

likelihood of future fatal crashes).[6] As a result, the offending airline suffers substantial, adverse financial consequences, *over and above* the costs of losing the plane and being sued on behalf of the victims. Although these research findings do not guarantee that airlines provide the efficient level of safety, they do reveal that the market punishes unsafe performance—suggesting a striking degree of safety awareness on the part of supposedly ignorant consumers. If consumers (who are, after all, the ultimate judges of the value of their own safety) can accurately and cheaply judge the *outcomes* of the safety procedures followed by airlines, ignorance about the *nature* of those procedures may be irrelevant to the provision of the efficient level of safety.

The final matter we consider is the potential impact of "excessive" competition on air safety.[7] Prior to 1978 the federal government—specifically, the Civil Aeronautics Board (CAB)—regulated the prices and routes of commercial airlines in the United States and also controlled new firms' entry into the industry. As a result of CAB regulation, the price of airline tickets was well above competitive levels, giving airlines an extra incentive to use "nonprice" measures—such as more numerous and more pleasant flight attendants and larger seats—to attract customers. One potential means of competing on a nonprice basis was to offer safer service. Once the industry was deregulated and prices fell to competitive levels, nonprice competition of all types would be expected to diminish, implying fewer and less pleasant attendants, narrower seats, and, possibly, less safety.

There is another force at work here, however. When the airlines were regulated, they had little to fear in the way of competition from other airlines; CAB regulations made it difficult for existing airlines to begin service on a new route, and

---

[6]Mark L. Mitchell and Michael T. Maloney, "Crisis in the Cockpit? The Role of Market Forces in Promoting Air Travel Safety," *Journal of Law and Economics*, October 1989, pp. 139–184.

[7]See Chapter 8 for a more extensive discussion of airline deregulation.

almost impossible for new airlines to enter the industry. Thus, under CAB regulation, an airline operating unsafely would not have to worry much about fearful customers switching to other, safer airlines.[8] Since 1978, however, existing and new airlines have been free to enter markets served by other airlines. We might expect this to put competitive pressure on airlines to operate more safely, since unsafe operations would send potential passengers scurrying to other airlines. Thus, the added competition that accompanied deregulation should have improved safety.

It is unclear which of these two conflicting forces (there may be more)—less nonprice competition or greater choice of airlines—would dominate. As it turns out, the net effect of deregulation on safety appears to have been negligible.[9] As discussed in Chapter 8, although there has been a rise in "near-misses" involving commercial airlines, most of this increase appears to be due to problems with the (government-operated) air traffic control system and with changes in reporting requirements, rather than to less safe behavior by airlines. Going in the other direction, airline fatalities per passenger miles have declined under deregulation, to 0.5 per billion passenger miles in 1979–86 from 1.2 per billion passenger miles in 1972–79. This move seems largely accounted for by a preexisting downward trend in fatalities over time, however, rather than by any significantly greater effort toward safety on the part of the airlines.

Oddly, however, there may have been one largely unexpected safety benefit resulting from airline deregulation. The lower prices of airline tickets under deregulation have induced more people to fly. Some of these people appear to have switched from driving to flying. Since flying on scheduled,

---

[8]Naturally, the airlines still had to worry about people switching to cars or trains, or simply not traveling at all; the point is that, under CAB regulation, one alternative—competing airlines—was less readily available.

[9]Richard B. McKenzie and William F. Shugart II, "Deregulation and Air Travel Safety," *Regulation*, Volume 11, nos. 3/4, 1987, pp. 42–47.

commercial airlines is roughly 100 times safer than driving, this switch in travel modes is estimated to have significantly reduced annual highway accidents, injuries, and deaths since 1978. Sometimes, fact really is stranger than fiction.

DISCUSSION QUESTIONS

1. Is it possible to be *too* safe? Explain what *you* mean by "too safe."
2. Many automobile manufacturers routinely advertise the safety of their cars, yet airlines generally do not even *mention* safety in their advertising. Can you suggest an explanation for this difference?

6

Choice and Life: The Economics of Abortion

The Supreme Court is back in the abortion business. For 16 years, the Court refused to substantively tamper with its 1973 *Roe v. Wade* decision legalizing abortion. But in 1989, in *Webster v. Reproductive Health Services*, the court upheld the constitutionality of a Missouri law restricting a woman's right to have an abortion.[1] Separately, the Court also announced its intention to hear other abortion cases posing even more fundamental issues than raised in the 1989 *Webster* decision. In anticipation of, and subsequent to, the *Webster* decision, citizens on both sides of the abortion issue prepared for a long and heated series of legislative battles over the issue of a woman's right to

---

[1]The Court upheld the constitutionality of Missouri statutes barring the expenditure of public funds on abortion and ordering doctors to perform fetal viability tests on women seeking abortions in midpregnancy or beyond.

choose, versus a fetus' right to live. It appears likely that at least a dozen states will respond to the *Webster* decision by limiting the legality of abortion, and that most of these limitations will become the subject of court battles. Thus, barring an unexpectedly swift and unequivocally sweeping pronouncement on the constitutionality of abortion per se, it seems certain that the Supreme Court will be deciding abortion cases long after you have finished reading this book.

Very few of the major issues of our time are purely economic, and abortion is no exception. Economics cannot answer the question of whether life begins at conception, at 24 weeks, or at birth. Nor can economics determine whether abortion should be permitted or proscribed. Economics cannot (as yet) even predict how the Supreme Court may ultimately rule on such issues. What economics *can* do, however, is demonstrate the striking and sometimes surprising implications of the Court's decisions on abortion—whatever those decisions may be.

Pregnancy termination has been practiced since ancient times, and any legal bars to abortion seem to have been based on the father's right to his offspring. English common law allowed abortion before quickening (when fetal movement is first evident), and there is some doubt whether abortion even after quickening was considered a crime. The American colonies retained the tradition of English common law until the changeover to state statutes at the adoption of the Constitution. In 1828, New York enacted an antiabortion statute that became a model for most other states. The statute declared that abortion before quickening was a misdemeanor and abortion after quickening second-degree manslaughter. In the late nineteenth century, the quickening distinction disappeared and the penalties for all abortions were increased.

Except under extreme circumstances (such as to protect the life of the mother), abortion remained generally illegal in this country until about 30 years ago, when a few states began to ease the conditions under which it was legal to perform an abortion. The gradual process of liberalization that state legislatures seemed to be following was suddenly disrupted in 1973 with the landmark Supreme Court decision in *Roe v. Wade*— which overruled all state laws prohibiting abortion before the last 3 months of pregnancy. In effect, the Court ruled that a woman's right to an abortion was constitutionally protected except during the last stages of pregnancy. There matters stood until the Supreme Court's 1989 decision in *Webster v. Reproductive Health Services*.[2]

Strictly speaking, the court's decision in *Webster* was narrowly focused; its direct impact will be to permit (but not require) states to restrict the circumstances under which abortion is legal. Although the *Webster* decision stops far short of overturning *Roe v. Wade*, many observers see it as a step (albeit a small one) in that direction, a step that is likely to be followed in subsequent legislative and Supreme Court decisions. Thus, to understand the economic consequences of the court's decision, it will be useful to examine the market for abortions during the period prior to *Roe v. Wade*.

Consider first the factors of cost and risk. During the early 1970s, an illegal—but otherwise routine—abortion by a reputable physician in the United States typically cost a minimum of $3000 (in 1989 dollars), and could run as high as $4000 in a major east coast city.[3] Following *Roe v. Wade*, these prices dropped sharply, and by the time of *Webster*, a routine legal abortion performed during the first three months of pregnancy cost only about $250.[4] In the early 1970s, more than 350,000 women were admitted to American hospitals *annually* with complications resulting from abortions, and it is estimated that more than 1000 women a year died from im-

[2]This is not to say that all was quiet on the abortion front during this period. Indeed, opponents of abortion made numerous attempts to amend the Constitition so as to either prohibit abortion or establish that abortion was solely the province of the states. All such attempts failed.

[3]All of the dollar amounts mentioned in this chapter are adjusted for inflation and expressed in terms of 1989 dollars, so as to make them comparable.

[4]More complicated abortions, performed as late as the fifth or sixth month of pregnancy, cost $800–1000 if done on an outpatient basis in a clinic, and $1200–1500 if performed in a hospital.

properly performed pregnancy terminations. Following the Court's 1973 decision, complications and deaths from pregnancy termination dropped sharply. In the late 1980s, it is estimated, significant physical complications occurred in less than 1 percent of all legal abortions, and deaths due to legal abortions were virtually unknown. In short, the legalization of abortion was associated with a drastic reduction in both the monetary costs and physical dangers of pregnancy termination. Why was such an association observed?

Let's begin by looking at who might be willing to perform an illegal abortion and the price at which she or he would be willing to perform it. A physician convicted of performing an illegal abortion faced not only criminal prosecution (and the associated costs of a legal defense), but also expulsion from the medical profession and the consequent lifetime loss of license and livelihood. In addition, the doctor may have had to endure ostracism by a community that regarded abortion as a criminal act. In short, the costs to a doctor of such a criminal conviction were enormous, and the greatest portion of the fee for an illegal abortion was simply compensation for bearing this potential cost.

It must be acknowledged, of course, that there were physicians who had strong moral convictions regarding a woman's right to abortion. Some were willing to absorb the risks of performing an illegal abortion at a substantially reduced fee of, say, $600–800. Nevertheless, such physicians were in a small minority and not easy to find. Consequently, most women were faced with the choice between either paying $3000 or more for an abortion, paying $400–600 to an unlicensed abortionist operating under unsanitary conditions, or simply doing without. And for those choosing back-alley abortionists, the consequences often included infection, subsequent hospitalization, and possibly even sterility; for some, the decision was fatal.

The illegality of abortions, of course, increased the cost of both supplying and obtaining information about them; in turn, this made decisions about whether to have an abortion and who should perform it more difficult, and increased the chances that whatever decision was made would be regretted. Information is never free, even in legalized activities, since it costs money to acquaint potential buyers with the location, quality, and price of a good or service. But in the case of an illegal activity, the provision of information is even more expensive. Abortionists could not advertise, and the more widely they let their availability be known, the more likely they were to be arrested. While some doctors unwilling to perform an abortion did refer patients to other, more willing physicians, the referral was itself illegal and therefore risky. There were other ways of obtaining information about the professional competence of an abortionist. But how reliable is, say, the local hairdresser or even a "friend of a friend?" Women seeking an abortionist thus were not able to inform themselves of all the possibilities without spending large amounts of money and time; and even having done so, many were left facing enormous uncertainty about the best path. Some ended up spending too much money; others exposed themselves to unnecessary risks; some might even have chosen not to have an abortion had they been fully informed of the potential risks.

The situation confronting women during the years prior to the legalization of abortion can be usefully categorized by considering three examples. Although the settings are stylized, they are representative of the nature of the choices involved, and the costs and risks of each.

First, there is a wealthy executive's wife who visits a travel agency that arranges a package tour of Japan. Included is round-trip airfare, an essentially risk-free procedure in that country (where abortions are legal), and several days of subsequent sightseeing. The price tag: $6000.

Next, let's look at how the wife of a young attorney earning $40,000 a year resolves her dilemma. She goes to her physician, who on the quiet refers her to a doctor willing to perform an illegal abortion in his office for $2000. The expense forces the couple to delay the purchase of their first home—but then so too would the cost of having the baby.

Then there is the situation of the wife of a blue-collar worker making $20,000 a year. Surreptitiously asking around, she finds out from an acquaintance that the local barber will do the abortion in a back room for $600—aspirins, but not antibiotics, included.

For the wife of the wealthy executive, both the risk and the financial burden are negligible; to be sure, the money could have been spent on an expensive bauble, but at least she got a trip to Japan in return. For the young lawyer and his wife, the financial burden is considerable; and if unpaid law school debts preclude either the physician-performed abortion or the cost of completing the pregnancy, the only alternative is the risk of the back-room abortionist. Finally, the blue-collar couple get the worst of both worlds: The abortionist's fee pushes them over their already-tight budget, and the woman risks hospitalization or worse.

The pattern suggested by these examples was borne out in the years preceding the legalization of abortion. Relatively few women had the resources permitting travel to a foreign country where abortion was both safe and legal, nor did many have access to the information needed to learn about and arrange such an undertaking. Somewhat larger numbers of women had established relationships with physicians who either would perform abortions or could refer them to other, willing doctors; and if they were fortunate, they then at least had the option of choosing between the higher expense of the physician or the greater risk of the unlicensed abortionist. For many women, however, the lack of readily available information about alternatives, combined with the high costs of a physician-performed abortion, meant that the back-room quack, and the attendant risk of crippling infection, was the only realistic means of terminating a pregnancy.

The statistics for New York City in the early 1960s support the plausibility of this argument: Private hospitals aborted one pregnant woman patient in 250; municipal hospitals, one in 10,000. The rate for whites was five times that for nonwhites and thirty times that for Puerto Ricans. Lower-income women simply were not having as many abortions performed by qualified physicians in suitable surroundings as were upper-income women; and, as we noted earlier, the result was hundreds of thousands of abortion-related complications, plus more than 1000 deaths each year.

The legalization of abortion in 1973 brought a relatively swift end to such outcomes. No longer faced with the risk of losing liberty and livelihood, thousands of physicians became willing to perform abortions. Even those who, for moral or religious reasons, were unwilling to terminate pregnancies could at least refer patients to other physicians without legal risk to themselves. Within a short time, properly equipped abortion clinics were established, and even in states requiring abortions to be performed in hospitals, women found a greatly increased range of options. Legalization thus produced an enormous increase in the supply of pregnancy termination services, which in turn had several consequences.

As in any market where there is an increase in supply, the price of abortions fell drastically; holding quality and safety constant, the price reduction was as much as 90 percent. The decline in the price of physician-supplied abortions to levels at or below those charged by back-alley abortionists quickly drove most of the quacks out of business. As a result, the safety of abortions increased dramatically; serious infections and deaths due to abortion are estimated to have declined by 50 percent within a year of *Roe v. Wade*, and have since become quite rare. Information about abortions, once available only "on the sly" and at considerable trouble and expense, became openly available. Women considering pregnancy termination could call their physician's office or simply look in the telephone book for information about local services. Moreover, not only was knowledge about the price, quality, and safety of abortion openly available, so too were counseling services about the potentially adverse psychological or emotional consequences of what, for many women, was a difficult and trying decision.

As would be expected, the lower price of abortion and the more widely available information about the procedure combined to bring about a large increase in the number of abortions performed in this country. During 1973, slightly over 700,000 legal abortions were performed in the United States, many of them in the aftermath of the Supreme Court's landmark decision. One early study concluded that of the legal abortions that took place in the year following *Roe v. Wade*, "well over half—most likely between two-thirds and three-fourths . . . were replacements for illegal abortions."[5] By 1981, 1.6 million legal abortions a year were being performed in the United States, a rate that stayed constant throughout the 1980s.

What then are the likely consequences of the Court's decision in *Webster*? In the short run, not much. To be sure, abortions in public facilities in Missouri are now illegal, and women in the later stages of pregnancy must undergo costly and risky tests regarding fetal viability before having an abortion. Thus, the Court's decision has increased the costs of pregnancy termination in Missouri. The results probably will be fewer abortions and, perhaps, some illegal abortions and the choice of more effective means of (prepregnancy) birth control. Nevertheless, there are good (albeit more expensive) substitutes available—abortions in private facilities or in neighboring states—so that the magnitude of these effects is likely to be small. If the Court goes beyond the step it took in *Webster*, and if very many states (successfully) impose additional restrictions on abortion, there will be a more noticeable return to the conditions that prevailed before 1973: Abortions will become more expensive and less frequent, and more of them will be performed illegally and less safely. And, as was the case before 1973, the burden of these consequences will be borne largely by women in the middle- and lower-income brackets.

We emphasized at the outset that the issues raised by abortion go far beyond the economic consequences, and that economics cannot, in any event, determine whether abortion should be permitted or proscribed. What economics can do— as we hope that we have shown—is to illustrate some of the

---

[5]June Skylar and Beth Berkov, "Abortion, Illegitimacy, and the American Birth Rate," *Science*, Vol. 185 (September 13, 1974), pp. 914ff.

consequences of the decision between "choice" and "life." Whether an understanding of those consequences can—or even should—play a role in making that decision is a matter we can only leave to the reader.

DISCUSSION QUESTIONS

1. Suppose you wished to predict which states will impose more restrictive conditions on abortions. What factors—for example, per capita income and average age of the population—would you take into account in making your predictions?
2. Before 1973, legal penalties generally were imposed on suppliers of abortion rather than on demanders. How might the effects of prohibiting abortion been different had legal penalties been imposed on demanders rather than on suppliers?

Part Two

Market
Structures

INTRODUCTION

Markets can take many forms. The standard market structures that are usually discussed are (1) pure competition, (2) **monopolistic competition**, (3) **oligopoly**, and (4) **monopoly**. In this part, examples of these market structures are given.

An example of the perfectly competitive market is the market for publicly traded shares of common stock. It can be argued that such a market is extremely efficient, with the result that it is extremely difficult to "make a killing" by trading in that market, particularly if one uses **public information**.

Government regulation and collusive agreements (called **cartels**) are common tools used by (otherwise competitive) firms in their efforts to achieve the profits of monopoly. Often, these efforts are less than completely successful, yielding monopolistic competition or oligopoly. The chapters on drugs, medicine, airlines, and international cartels illustrate the many gradations possible. The chapters on medical costs, drug regulation, and the savings and loan industry also reveal that well-intentioned government policies sometimes have surprising consequences when they alter the incentives that normally operate in all markets.

One point should be kept in mind throughout this part: We are presenting models of human behavior, not of thought processes. Our analysis of the medical profession, for example, cannot be proved or disproved by asking physicians whether they think along the lines of our analysis. Our models are set up using an "as if" framework. That is to say, we assume that the individuals under study are acting as if they were attempting to maximize their self-interest.

7

A Random Walk Down Wall Street

Want to get rich quick? We know of only two sure ways:

1. Marry a wealthy person.
2. Buy low and sell high.

Based on the authors' experiences, we can't help you much with the first method; but we may be able to help you with the second.

Let's begin with the financial pages—sometimes called the business section—of the daily newspaper. There you will find column after column of information about the stocks and bonds of America's corporations. A share of **stock** in a corporation is simply a legal claim to a share of the corporation's future profits; owners of stocks are called **shareholders**. Thus, if there are 100,000 shares of stock in a company and you—as a shareholder—own 1000 of them, then you own the right to 1 percent of that company's future profits.

A **bond** is a legal claim against a firm, entitling the bond owner to received a fixed annual "coupon" payment, plus a lump sum payment at the bond's maturity date.[1] Bonds are issued in return for funds lent to the firm. The coupon payments represent interest on the amount borrowed by the firm, and the lump sum payment at maturity generally equals the amount originally borrowed. Bonds are *not* claims to the future profits of the firm; legally, the owners of the bonds—called *bondholders*—are to be paid whether the firm prospers or not.[2]

Now, suppose that in your quest for riches, you decide to buy some shares of stock in a corporation. How should you choose which corporation's stock to buy? One way is to consult a specialist in stocks, called a *stockbroker*. Such brokers have access to an enormous amount of information. They can tell you what lines of business specific corporations are in, who the firms' major competitors are, how profitable the firms have been in the past, and whether their stocks' prices have risen or fallen. If pressed, they probably will be willing to recommend which stocks to buy. Throughout, any brokers opinion will sound highly informed and authoritative.

Strange as it may seem, though, a broker's investment advice is not likely to be any better than anyone else's. In fact, *the chances of the broker's being right are no greater than the chances of your being right*! Indeed, on the average you are just as likely to get rich by throwing darts at the financial pages of your newspaper. Let's see why.

---

[1]Coupon payments on bonds get their name from the fact that bonds once had coupons attached to them when issued. Each year, the owner would clip a coupon off the bond and send it to the issuing firm in return for that year's interest.

[2]To ensure this, bondholders generally must receive their coupon payments each year, plus any principal due, before *any* shareholders can receive their share of the firm's profits—called *dividends*.

In 1967, the editors of the busines magazine *Forbes* taped the financial pages of a major newspaper to a wall and threw darts at the portion listing stock prices. They hit the stocks of 28 different companies and invested a hypothetical $1000 in each. By 1984 (when the editors halted their experiment), the original $28,000 had grown to $132,000—a gain of 370 percent. Over the same period, the Dow Jones Industrial Average (a leading measure of the stock market's overall performance) grew less than 40 percent in value. Perhaps even more impressive, *Forbes'* random selection of stocks outperformed the recommended stock portfolios of most of the "gurus" of stock market forecasting.

More recently, the editors of *The Wall Street Journal*, a major financial newspaper, tried a similar experiment. Each month they invited four stockbrokers to recommend a stock to buy; the four stocks became the "experts' **portfolio**" for the month. Then the editors threw four darts at the financial pages of their newspaper to select four stocks that became the "darts' portfolio" for the month. Over time, the particular expert brokers changed, depending on how well their picks performed relative to the darts' portfolio. Any broker whose stock beat the darts got to pick again the next month. Any expert beaten by the darts was replaced the next month by a new broker. After six months, the newspaper tallied up the performances of the experts versus the darts. If you had invested $1000 in each of the experts' picks, you would have ended up with $25,488. Had you invested $1000 in each of the darts' picks, you would have wound up with $24,816. Although the experts beat the darts in this head-to-head contest, the winning margin was fully accounted for by the performance of just *one* of the brokers; the darts actually *outperformed* a clear majority of the experts. How did the darts do it?

Suppose that you, and you alone, noticed that the price of a particular stock moved in a predictable manner. Specifically, assume the price *rose* 5 percent on even-numbered days and *fell* 5 percent on odd-numbered days, resulting in (approximately) no average change over time. Knowing this fact, how do you make money? You simply buy shares of the stock just before it is due to rise, and sell shares of the stock just before it is due to fall. If you start the year with $1000 and reinvest your profits, following this strategy would yield profits in excess of $500,000 by the end of the year. And *if* you continue this strategy for a second year, your wealth would exceed $250 million!

Of course, as your wealth accumulates—"buying low and selling high"—your purchases and sales would start to affect the price of the stock. In particular, your purchases would drive the low prices up and your sales would drive high prices down. Ultimately, your buying and selling in response to predictable patterns would *eliminate* those patterns, and there would be no profit potential left to exploit. This is *exactly* what happens in the stock market—except it happens far faster than a single person could accomplish it alone.

At any point in time, there are tens of thousands—perhaps millions—of persons looking for any bit of information that will help them forecast the future prices of stocks. Responding to any information that seems useful, these people try to "buy low and sell high." As a result, all publicly available information that might be used to forecast stock prices gets taken into account—leaving no predictable profits. And, since there are so many people involved in this process, it occurs quite swiftly. Indeed, there is evidence that *all* information entering the market is *fully incorporated* into stock prices within *less than a minute* of its arrival.[3]

The result is that stock prices tend to follow a **random walk**—which is to say that the best forecast of tomorrow's price is today's price, plus a random component. And, although large values of the random component are less likely than small values, nothing else about its magnitude or sign (positive or negative) can be predicted. Indeed, the random component of stock prices exhibits behavior much like what

---

[3]See L. J. Feinstone, "Minute by Minute: Efficiency, Normality and Randomness in Intra-Daily Asset Prices," *Journal of Applied Econometrics* 2 (1987), 193–214.

would occur if you rolled two dice and subtracted seven from the resulting score. *On average,* the dice will total 7, so after you subtract 7, the average result will be zero. It is true that rolling a 12 or a 2 (yielding a net score of $+5$ or -5) is less likely than rolling an 8 or a 6 (producing a net score of $+1$ or -1). Nevertheless, positive and negative net scores are equally likely, and the expected net score is zero.[4]

It is worth emphasizing that the bond market operates every bit as efficiently as the stock market. That is, investors in bonds study the available information and use whatever might help them forecast future bond prices. And since they exploit this information up to the point that the benefits of doing so are just matched by the costs, there remains *no* publicly available information that can profitably be used to improve bond price forecasts. As a result, bond prices, like stock prices, follow a random walk. Moreover, since interest rates are inextricably linked to the prices of bonds, interest rates, too, follow a random walk.

In light of the foregoing, two questions arise. First, are all the efforts put into forecasting stock and bond prices simply a waste? The answer is no. From a social viewpoint, this effort is productive because it helps ensure that asset prices correctly reflect all available information, and thus that resources are efficiently allocated. From a private standpoint, the effort is rewarding too, just as any other productive activity is rewarding. At the margin, the gains from trying to forecast future stock and bond prices are exactly equal to the costs of doing so; there are no unexploited profit opportunities. Unless you happen to have some unique ability that makes you better than others, you will earn only enough to cover your costs—but of course the same is true of growing wheat or selling women's

---

[4]Strictly speaking, stock prices follow a random walk with "drift"; that is, on average they rise at a real (inflation-adjusted) rate of about 3 percent per year over long periods of time. This drift, which is the average compensation investors receive for deferring consumption, can be thought of as the 7 that comes up on average when two dice are rolled.

shoes. So, absent some special ability, you are just as well off investing in the market based on the roll of the dice—or the throw of a dart.

The second question is a bit trickier: Isn't there *any* way to "beat the market?" The answer is yes—but only if you have **inside information**, i.e., information unavailable to the public. Suppose, for example, that your best friend is in charge of new product development for Mousetrap Inc., a firm that just last night invented a mousetrap superior to all others on the market. No one but your friend—and now you—are aware of this. You could indeed make money with this information, by purchasing shares of Mousetrap Inc. and then selling them (at a higher price) as soon as the invention is publicly announced. There is one problem: Stock trading based on such inside information is normally illegal, punishable by substantial fines and even imprisonment. So, unless you happen to have a stronger-than-average desire for a long vacation in a federal prison, our money-making advice to you is simple: Invest in the mousetrap after it hits the market—and throw darts in the meantime.

DISCUSSION QUESTIONS

1. Why do you think the government prohibits insider trading?
2. Can you think of any other assets whose prices might follow random walks?

8

Better Late Than Never:
The Economics of
Airline Delays

This is a "good news/bad news" story. First the good news: Since 1978, the price of airline tickets in the United States has plummeted; as a result, America is becoming the land of frequent flyers. People who once flew only on business are taking to the air for vacation trips as well. Millions of Americans who had never flown before are "super-saving" on coast-to-coast flights as though they were born to it. For many people, the annual debate over a trip to the beach or a trip to the mountains focuses today on the merits of the surf at Waikiki versus the scenery of the Swiss Alps.

Now the bad news: Except for flights on the very longest routes, "air travel" is often spent mostly on the ground—getting into and through the departure airport; checking baggage; waiting for delayed planes to arrive at the gate; sitting on the tarmac as the plane awaits permission to take off; battling crowds to retrieve baggage; and getting through and out of one's arrival airport. Even in the air, if one is flying into a busy airport such as Chicago's O'Hare or New York's LaGuardia, much of flight time may be occupied with the plane's inscribing precision rectangles through the air, awaiting clearance to land.

In short, Americans today are flying more because they are paying less. Yet for many air travelers, much of the savings on ticket prices are squandered on waiting time. Why is this so, and what might be done about it?

Most people know that Orville and Wilbur Wright inaugurated heavier-than-air flight on a windy December afternoon in 1903. Fewer know that three decades later, just as commercial air travel was getting off the ground (so to speak) the U.S. government sought to permanently suppress competition among the nation's fledgling airlines.[1] In 1935, the federal government established the Civil Aeronautics Board (CAB), a government agency whose avowed purpose was to ensure the long-run survival of commercial air travel in this country by preventing "ruinous competition" among airlines. In fact, the true purpose of the CAB was to facilitate and enforce a cartel among established airlines, so as to enhance the profitability of those firms. Over the next 40 years, the CAB pursued this objective along three major margins. First, with but a few trivial exceptions, the agency forbade the entry of new firms into the business of providing scheduled, interstate airline service.[2] Second, when two or more airlines served the same route, the CAB sharply limited the ability of those airlines to compete on the basis of cheaper ticket prices. Third, the agency largely prevented carriers from initiating flights on

---

[1]The steps taken by the U.S. government were soon followed by most other governments of the world with regard to their own nations' airlines.

[2]Airlines that operate only *intra*state scheduled service, e.g., between San Francisco and Los Angeles, were not subject to CAB regulation but were typically regulated to some degree by similar state agencies.

routes already served by one or more other airlines. In each instance, the overriding goal of the CAB was to keep airfares above the competitive level, thereby enhancing airline profitability.[3]

The CAB had been founded to prop up airfares at a time of deflation (the Great Depression), when the prices of all goods and services had been falling at record rates. During the 1970s, inflation was the chief problem facing the U.S. economy, and many politicians felt that promoting competition in the airline industry would bring about beneficially lower airfares. There was also growing evidence that the purely intrastate airlines of California and Texas, which had developed free of CAB regulation, were providing comparable service at much lower fares than charged by the regulated interstate airlines.[4] Many consumers had thus come to regard the CAB as a classic example of wasteful regulation on the part of the government. The combination of these growing sentiments led in 1978 to deregulation of the U.S. airline industry: CAB control over fares, routes, and entry was phased out, and provision was made for the ultimate abolition of the CAB (which finally took place in 1985).

The ensuing outbreak of competition among U.S. airlines was nothing short of staggering. Airfares were slashed,

---

[3]There is one seeming exception to this policy of unabashed devotion to the enhancement of airline profits: The CAB forced scheduled airlines to provide service for numerous small cities at prices that were below the full costs of the service. Such cities tended to be the home of members of Congress (who determined the size of the CAB's budget) or of constituents important to those members of Congress. Hence such subsidization may be viewed as the political "payoff" required to ensure the success of the CAB's other efforts to enhance airline profits.

[4]For example, in 1974, Pacific Southwest Airlines offered a Los Angeles–San Francisco fare of $19, compared to $41 charged on the CAB-regulated, but otherwise comparable, Boston–Washington route. Similarly, Southwest offered $15 off-peak and $25 peak fares intrastate between Dallas and Houston, while CAB-regulated carriers charged 28 percent more on the same route.

existing airlines began service on new routes, and there was a massive influx of new airlines. During the first five years of deregulation, the number of U.S. airlines rose to 123 from 36, an increase of more than 225 percent. Lucrative transcontinental and transoceanic routes, once reserved by the CAB for only a few select airlines, soon were being served by a dozen or more carriers on each. "Super-saver" fares, which offer hefty price discounts in return for advance ticket purchases and other travel restrictions, had been carefully restricted by the CAB; by the late 1980s, more than 90 percent of all airline passengers were traveling on super-saver tickets. Frequent-flyer programs, offering "free" tickets and service upgrades (e.g., from coach to first class) in return for past travel on an airline, became commonplace.

The competition spurred by the deregulation of the airline industry has brought ticket prices to record-low levels. Despite the fact that prices overall have nearly *doubled* since 1978, the average cost of an airline ticket has actually *declined*. Thus, measured in today's dollars, a "typical" one-way airline ticket that sold for $200 in 1978 now goes for only about $100. Not surprisingly, consumers have responded to the lower relative price of air travel by flying more. In 1988, U.S. airlines carried more than 460 million passengers, up from 240 million a decade earlier—an increase almost the size of the entire U.S. population. In a 1988 report, the U.S. Federal Trade Commission estimated that deregulation had saved American consumers more than $100 *billion* since its inception. Currently, it is estimated that lower airfares are continuing to save consumers about $12 billion annually.

The early years of deregulation were, from the consumer's standpoint, a period of unalloyed improvement. Better service, greater choice, and lower fares combined to make air travel the best deal in town. By the mid-1980s, however, problems had begun to surface. To some, indeed, airline deregulation was becoming a victim of its own success. By opening up air travel to millions of Americans, deregulation was straining the capacity of U.S. airports and airways. The results became commonplace: delayed and cancelled flights, missed connections, overburdened air traffic controllers, and airports jammed with holiday-size crowds every day. At some major airports, the cancellation rate on scheduled flights was running at 10 percent. Departure and arrival delays became so frequent that the federal government was ultimately pressured into releasing the on-time records of scheduled airlines. And when the statistics revealed that the major carriers were routinely late 25–40 percent of the time, the airlines responded by simply rewriting their schedules to make their performance appear better. Air traffic controllers, whose ranks had been thinned by mass firings during their abortive 1981 strike, found themselves handling 50 percent more commercial flights with 25 percent fewer personnel. At major airports, the controllers were further burdened by aging equipment that was a decade or more out-of-date. As a result, "near misses" involving commercial airliners rose to record-high levels.

Some angry travelers have responded to these developments by arguing that the United States should return to federal regulation of the airline industry. To be sure, the outcome of such a move would be less air travel congestion, because regulation's higher airfares and reduced service levels would ensure that outcome. But such a move would also impose billions of dollars of costs on consumers each year, as they would be forced to pay higher ticket prices, travel less, and choose less-preferred modes of transportation. Many economists would argue that there is a superior method of relieving air travel congestion, one that involves not *reregulation*, but instead *more deregulation*. How can this be?

Air travel involves three essential components: airlines, airports, and airways. The 1978 legislation abolishing CAB control deregulated only airlines. The basic structure of airports and the airways (principally, the air traffic control system) was left unchanged—which is to say, almost exclusively under government control. Thus, privately owned airlines were given both the opportunity and the incentives to expand air travel, and they responded vigorously—cutting prices, buying new planes, adding routes, hiring pilots and other personnel, and so forth. Government-operated airports and airways were given neither the opportunity nor the incentive to respond similarly, and so they did not. The outcome in air travel is exactly what would happen with automobile transportation if a two-lane road were expanded to eight lanes *except* at two points, where it remained two lanes. Initially, traffic would increase to take advantage of the expanded eight-lane service, but ultimately traffic flow would be limited by the bottlenecks created by the remaining two-lane segments. This is exactly what happened when airlines were deregulated; service expanded but is now constrained by the bottlenecks created by the airport and airway systems. Until the nation's airports and airways are somehow "deregulated," possibly by transferring their operation to private hands, flight delays and cancellations, overcrowded airports, and midair near-misses will only get worse.

Consider first the air traffic control system. Virtually all commercial air traffic controllers are employees of the Federal Aviation Administration (FAA), a U.S. government agency. Thus, controllers are subject to federal civil service regulations that are better suited for slow-paced paper movement than for the rapidly changing world of airline travel. Among other things, FAA controllers of a given grade are required to receive the same pay, whether they work in the high-stress environment of Chicago's busy O'Hare Airport or in the almost-sleepy control tower at the Greenville-Spartanburg Airport in South Carolina.[5] It is little wonder that the FAA has had enormous difficulty keeping its staffs at busy airports at anything close to full strength.

In a similar vein, physical air traffic control facilities, both at airports (controlling takeoffs and landings) and at enroute traffic control centers (controlling the movement of planes be-

---

[5]The FAA has recently announced plans to experiment with a 25 percent pay bonus for controllers working at high-stress airports such as O'Hare.

tween airports) are owned by the FAA. As such, the acquisition of all equipment is subject to cumbersome federal procurement policies. The serious delays caused by these policies are well illustrated by the FAA's "National Airspace System Plan," a 10-year project begun in 1983 to modernize the air traffic control system. As early as 1987, key parts of the plan were already four years behind schedule. Moreover, a recent U.S. Secretary of Transportation has publicly admitted that by the time the system is finally in place, most of its computers and other components will be "technological relics." In 1988, lack of modern equipment at O'Hare Airport forced the FAA to cut peak-level flights there from 96 an hour to 80 an hour, a move that ended up disrupting air traffic throughout the country.

Both the personnel and procurement processes of the air traffic control system are further hampered by the fact that the system is part of the overall federal budget process. Since funding for the system comes chiefly from federal taxes on airline tickets and aviation fuel, all spending on air traffic control must be authorized and appropriated by Congress. As a result, the size and structure of the air traffic control system is more likely to be determined by the latest federal deficit "crisis," or the current membership of Congressional budget committess, than by the airlines and air travelers who use the system.

Some observers argue that many of these problems could be avoided if the air traffic control system were turned over to the private sector. For example, since 1972 Britain has permitted airports to operate their local traffic control operations (for takeoffs and landings) as they see fit—by running the operations themselves, contracting operations out to private firms, or paying government controllers to handle takeoffs and landings. It has even been suggested that enroute traffic control (for planes between airports) could be handled by the private sector, owned perhaps by a consortium of airlines, airports, pilots, and the like. In principle, at least, private ownership of the air traffic control system would enable its owners to respond quickly and efficiently to changing cost-and-demand conditions in the industry, much as privately owned airlines have done under deregulation.

Critics of any plan for a private air traffic control system have questioned whether the private sector would offer the same level of safety as the current, government-controlled system. Some have argued, for example, that private owners would be more concerned with profits than with safety. Such criticism ignores several important points, however. First, U.S. airlines are already operated by the private sector, and they have compiled an admirable safety record over the past half century or so.[6] There is no reason the think that the private sector would fail to do likewise if it operated the airways. Second, private operation of the airways does not preclude government involvement in setting and enforcing safety standards, just as the FAA currently does with airlines. Finally, as we just noted, the British long have left airport traffic control decisions in the hands of airport operators; the success of this system has been good enough to prompt serious discussion in Britain of turning enroute air traffic control over to the private sector as well. The British experience strongly suggests that private air traffic control could be successful in America.

Whatever measures are taken to relieve congestion of the airways, there remains the problem of overcrowded airports. Virtually all airports used by scheduled airlines in America are owned by government authorities, typically local governments or consortia of local and state governments. As such, they are generally not operated on a for-profit basis, and so

---

[6]The vast increase in the number of Americans flying has heightened interest in airline safety. The media has responded by devoting more prominent news coverage to airplane crashes and nonfatal "incidents," such as jammed landing gear and near-misses. The resulting headlines give the impression that flying has become riskier. In fact, airline safety, measured in terms of fatalities per passenger-mile, has improved markedly over the past 15 years—continuing a trend that dates back to the inception of scheduled airline service.

have less incentive to respond efficiently to changing economic conditions. Although government ownership is not an absolute bar to economically efficient operation, several examples illustrate that it has acted as such in the case of airports.

First, there is the matter of the pricing of airport services. Planes wishing to land at airports must pay landing fees. Currently, these fees are based almost exclusively on the *weight* of the aircraft, with heavier planes paying higher fees. The rationale is that heavier planes "use" more of the airport's facilities, because they place greater physical stresses on the runways and are likely to be occupied by more passengers using the terminal facilities. This type of pricing ignores both (1) the value placed on landing by the owners and occupants of the plane and (2) the cost that one plane's landing imposes on other planes by making them wait.

In effect, the current weight-based system of landing fees is much like a pricing scheme in which restaurant patrons were charged a price for their meal based on their weight rather than on what they consumed. One can easily imagine the consequences: Restaurants would immediately be overpopulated by very hungry, slender people who would order enormous amounts of the most expensive menu entries and then spend an inordinate amount of time consuming their meal. This is roughly what has happened with airports. A small private plane pays as little as $25 to land at some major commercial airports, even during the airports' busiest times. As a result, fully loaded jumbo jets are sometimes forced to delay landing, in each instance imposing several hundreds (or perhaps thousands) of dollars in costs on the airlines owning the jumbo jets and the passengers occupying them. Since the operators of light planes are not required to bear these costs, the result is "too many" private aircraft landing at major airports. Just as private restaurants in fact charge their patrons based on the value of the items consumed, presumably so too would private operators of airports. The result would be higher fees for small aircraft landing at major airports. Many would thus choose to land at outlying airports, thereby reducing the delays faced by scheduled airline passengers.[7]

Government-operated airports also price inefficiently over the course of each day. Many passengers (and thus airlines) seem to prefer departures and landings between the hours of 7:00 A.M. and 10:00 A.M. and again between 4:00 P.M. and 7:00 P.M., presumably because these times roughly correspond to the beginning and end of the business workday. These busiest times of the day are referred to as peak-load periods, and similar types of peak-load periods are observed in many lines of business, including restaurants, movie theaters, and telephone services. In general, since it is demand during peak periods that determines the maximum capacity required of an airport, restaurant, or telephone system, it is economically efficient (and more profitable) to charge consumers a higher price for services rendered during peak periods. Privately owned companies typically do just this, and the higher peak-load prices (such as higher long-distance rates during the day than at night) help reduce peak-period consumption, and thus reduce the (costly) nuisance of peak congestion. By contrast, government-owned airports generally charge the same landing fees regardless of the time of day; this results in excessive congestion during peak periods, and thus departure and arrival delays and cancellations. Having privately owned airports, whose owners presumably would price their services like private owners of other businesses facing peak periods, would alleviate much of this congestion.

Although the idea of private, for-profit airports may sound strange, there are numerous small private airports in the United States, and even a large private airport in Burbank, California, (operated by Lockheed) that serves commercial air-

---

[7]Naturally, just as normally light eaters sometimes choose to treat themselves to large meals at expensive restaurants, the owners of small aircraft—occupied, say, by the chief executives of major corporations—might well choose to land at busier, more convenient airports. This creates no inefficiency so long as those aircraft pay the full cost of their landings.

lines. Moreover, in 1987 the British government privatized the British Airports Authority, which is now a for-profit, shareholder-owned firm that owns and operates most major British airports, including London's Heathrow and Gatwick airports. So far, owners and users alike have been pleased with the new arrangement.

Adding to the congestion problems of government-owned airports in the United States has been the heavy hand of the FAA. For example, the authority operating Boston's congested Logan Airport recently wished to experiment with high landing fees during peak periods, in the hope of reducing delays. The FAA objected, however, and the airport was forced to abandon the plan.

Even more important, the FAA controls the allocation of takeoff and landing "slots" at major commercial airports. It decides how many slots will be available at each airport, and what proportion of the slots shall go to scheduled airlines and what to "general aviation" (such as private and corporate aircraft). After making these decisions, the FAA then *gives* the slots away in lotteries, despite their high market value. A slot is worth $400,000 at Washington, D.C., National Airport, $300,000 at O'Hare, and $200,000 and $100,000, respectively, at New York's LaGuardia and Kennedy airports.[8] If the FAA *sold* the slots instead of just handing them out, it could raise billions of dollars to speed modernization of the nation's aging air traffic control system. Alternatively, the FAA could allow *airports* to sell the slots, a move that would provide a major new source of funding for terminal and runway expansion, as well as incentives to build more airports. The last major new airport in the United States opened in 1974 at Dallas–Ft. Worth, and only two major airports have engaged in significant expansions since deregulation. And even with the congestion problems faced at airports across the country, only two cities—Denver, Colorado, and Austin, Texas—currently have

---

[8]Airlines are allowed to buy existing slots from one another but are not allowed to buy slots from the pool assigned to general aviation.

plans for new airports. Federal constraints such as the FAA's slot-allocation policy have sharply curtailed funding sources for modernized facilities and new airports, further adding to congestion in the skies.

By stimulating competition, the 1978 deregulation of U.S. airlines has brought down airfares and thus greatly expanded opportunities for air travel. Yet unless U.S. airports and airways are themselves relieved of government controls, the benefits of airline deregulation will be smaller and often more exasperating than they could be. For those persons currently waiting for a plane to take off or land—some of whom might never have flown without deregulation—we can offer only a reminder of this old adage: Better late than never.

DISCUSSION QUESTIONS

1. Why do you think the government gives away landing slots rather than sells them?
2. Why do you think the FAA objected to the plan to begin peak-load pricing of landing slots at Boston's Logan Airport?
3. Is it possible that the waiting costs under deregulation are greater than the savings from the lower ticket prices due to deregulation? (Hint: What has happened to the amount of air travel?)

9

The Two-Edged Sword
of Drug Regulation

Medical drugs are a two-edged sword. If they are carefully manufactured, appropriate for curing your illness, and free of side effects, your pain and suffering may be prevented, or at least assuaged, and your life may even be saved. If, on the other hand, the drug you take under your doctor's supervision turns out to have side effects, you may be worse off than if you had never taken the drug at all, or if you had taken an alternative drug without side effects.

Federal regulation has been concerned not only with the safety, but also with the efficacy—the effectiveness—of drugs for many years. The first federal legislation, the Food and Drug Act of 1906, dealt with adulteration and misbranding, with safety being covered under the adulteration section. That act prohibited inclusion of any substance that would be poisonous or harmful to health. To some extent, the act was successful. Dr. Hostatter's celebrated Stomach Bitters and Kickapoo Indian Sagwa, along with numerous rum-laden concoctions, cocaine-based potions, and supposed anticancer remedies, disappeared from the alchemists' shelves as a result of this legislation. The original act was expanded in 1938 with the passage of the federal Food, Drug, and Cosmetic Act, which forced manufacturers to demonstrate the safety of new drugs. It resulted from public reaction to the deaths of 107 individuals who had taken an elixir of sulfanilamide, which just happened to include diethylene glycol, a poisonous substance usually used as antifreeze.

The next step in drug regulation came after the birth of numerous deformed infants whose mothers had been taking a sleeping pill called Thalidomide. At the time that these deformities became apparent, the drug was widely used in Europe, and the Food and Drug Administration (FDA) was moving toward approving Thalidomide in the United States. In fact, about two-and-a-half million Thalidomide tablets were in the hands of U.S. physicians as samples. At the insistence of President Kennedy, the FDA removed all of the samples. Using the Thalidomide incident as ammunition, Senator Estes Kefauver secured passage of his bill, known as the 1962 Kefauver-Harris Amendments to the 1938 Food, Drug, and Cosmetic Act. Kefauver and his associates wished to prevent, among other things, a proliferation of new drugs.

Prior to the 1962 amendments, the FDA normally approved a new drug application within a 180-day time limit, unless the application did not adequately demonstrate during that time that the drug was safe for use as suggested in the proposed labeling. The 1962 amendments added a "proof of efficacy" requirement and removed the time constraint on the FDA. Thus, since 1962, it has been the case that no drug can be marketed unless and until the FDA determines that it is safe and effective in its intended use.

Let's reiterate here what is at issue. The FDA enforces legislation so that two things are prevented: (1) the marketing of unsafe drugs, and (2) the proliferation of drugs that are "unnecessary," in the sense that the drugs do not do what they purport to do. Consumers presumably are better protected by this legislation because generally they do not have the ability to obtain (let alone fully analyze) the information necessary to make an accurate choice about the safety or efficacy of a particular drug. They are, in a sense, at the mercy of their physicians. But their physicians are also, in a sense, at the mercy of the drug companies. Physicians cannot possibly keep up with all the technical literature about drugs and be aware of the differences among them.

To keep the medical profession informed, drug companies spend thousands of dollars a year per physician. They send out so-called detail people to inform physicians of new drugs and to give them samples to dispense to patients so doctors can find out for themselves how effective the drugs really are. To be sure, doctors, hospitals, and drug companies do have an incentive to prescribe, market, and produce safe drugs. After all, if it can be proven that side effects from drug use cause harm to an individual, the ensuing lawsuit will certainly make the doctor, hospital, or manufacturer worse off. Additionally, the negative publicity surrounding such a lawsuit will not enhance the future reputation of the drug company involved. And finally, the more lawsuits filed and won by injured parties, the higher the total cost of drug production and the higher the price ultimately paid by the consumer. Since the law of demand applies to medical drugs, the resultant higher price to the consumer will cause a reduction in the quantity of drugs demanded.

The 1962 amendments seem to have been very effective in reducing the number of new drugs introduced into the medical marketplace. In fact, several researchers have estimated that the 1962 law cut new drug introductions in the United States by as much as two-thirds. That should not be surprising. The cost of introducing a new drug has risen dramatically. Prior to the 1962 amendments, the average time between filing and approval of a new drug application was 7 months; by 1967, it was 30 months; and currently it takes 8–10 years for a new drug to be approved by the FDA. In other words, the 1962 amendments have resulted in extending the period during which new drugs must be continuously tested. In making investment decisions, firms are keenly aware of this additional cost, and so they have cut new drug introductions in this country.

The effect has been what some people call the U.S. drug lag. The number of drugs marketed in England that are not available in the United States, for example, is very much larger than the reverse situation. Although the FDA and its supporters note that it takes time to ensure that patients are benefited rather than harmed by new drugs, regulation-induced drug lag can itself be life-threatening. Dr. George Hitchings, a winner of the Nobel Prize in medicine, has estimated that the five-year lag in introducing Septra (an antibacterial agent) to the United States "killed 100,000, maybe a million people" in this country. Similarly, a class of drugs called beta blockers (used to treat heart attack victims and people with high blood pressure) was introduced nearly a decade later in this country than in Europe. According to several researchers, the lag in the FDA appoval of these drugs cost the lives of at least 250,000 Americans.

Now we come to the realization that for every benefit, there seems to be a cost. Clearly, there is a dollar cost to the drug companies in testing more completely the efficacy and safety of a drug. But if that were the only issue, there probably wouldn't be many critics of the FDA. The reason there are so many critics of the FDA today is the cost to individuals who could be better off if the introduction of so many drugs had not been delayed or prevented since 1962.

Let's now consider the safety problem in total. Every time a new drug is introduced, it has potentially harmful side effects. Thus, part of the cost of introducing that drug is the cost of the undesired side effects to those affected by them. This is called a "Type I error." It is the probability of introducing a drug that should not have been introduced. Since 1962, we have reduced the Type I error—the Thalidomide possibility—by increasing the amount of testing necessary for the introduction of new drugs. People have undoubtedly benefited by this reduction in Type I error by incurring fewer side effects. But other people have been hurt. They have been the victims of what is called a "Type II error." Their cost is the pain, suffering, and possible death that occur because of the lack of availability of a drug that *would have been offered* on the marketplace in the absence of the 1962 amendments. The Type II error, then, is the probability of not introducing a new drug that should have been introduced. To understand better the cost of a Type II error, consider the possiblity of the 1962 drug amendments' being applied to aspirin. It is very hard to demonstrate *why* aspirin is effective—and it may have bad side effects, such as duodenal ulcers, if taken often. Imagine, though, if it had never been introduced. What would the cost have been? People would have incurred more pain from headaches, arthritis, and so on. In other words, the Type II error cost is the pain and suffering that occur because a drug was *not* introduced.

In some cases, the FDA has shortened the testing period for drugs in cases where Type I errors are insignificant compared to type II errors—as is the case with terminally ill individuals. Since the mid-1970s, the FDA has approved several drugs on the basis of a shorter testing period for use in the treatment of patients with terminal diseases. A vaccine for use in the treatment of AIDS (acquired immune deficiency syndrome) emerged in 1986 and received tentative FDA approval after only an 18-month testing period. When it was found that azidothymidine (AZT) prolonged the lives of patients with AIDS, it was felt that the possible side effects of the drug (Type I errors)—such as headaches, nausea, and a reduction in the number of disease-fighting white blood cells—were far outweighed by the many deaths (Type II errors) that would result if the drug weren't quickly approved.

Recently, the FDA has also shortened the period of time necessary for the approval of **generic drugs**. In cases where a generic drug is of essentially the same composition as a drug formerly approved and marketed under a brand name, upon expiration of the patent held by the original producer the FDA allows the drug to be marketed under its generic name with little further testing. Despite this new policy and the FDA's expedited review of AZT, most of the agency's critics remain convinced of one conclusion: The FDA has too often and for too long allowed the two-edged sword of drug regulation to fall on patients instead of on their diseases.

DISCUSSION QUESTIONS

1. Does the type of market structure in which drugs are produced have anything to do with the tradeoff between Type I and Type II errors? In other words, would our analysis be different if the drug industry were either perfectly competitive or a pure monopoly?
2. On the whole, do you feel longer FDA testing periods for drugs have increased or reduced the amount of pain and suffering experienced in the United States?

10

Up, Up, and Away: The Rising Costs of Medical Care

Most people don't have to be told about how expensive it is these days to see a doctor or go into a hospital. If we compare the **Consumer Price Index** (CPI) with a medical care price index, we see that since 1967 the CPI has increased by 300 percent, while the medical care index has risen by 450 percent. The rising relative cost of medical care has contributed to Americans' spending a record-high share of their total incomes on medical care. We spent only $40 billion on medical care in 1965; today we spend over $500 billion each year. Even after adjusting for inflation, this means that spending on medical care has more than tripled since 1965. Twenty-five years ago, expenditures on medical care amounted to less than 7 percent of total national expenditures, but today's medical expenditures represent over 11 percent of total spending.[1] The rising cost of medical care is likely to be one of the most expensive and explosive issues faced in the coming decade.

If we wish to understand why medical care has become so expensive, we have to look at a number of factors. They include (1) past restrictions on the supply of physicians, (2) increases in demand created by Medicare and Medicaid, (3) increases in the quantity of care demanded due to third-party insurance, and (4) soaring medical malpractice insurance costs and resultant increases in so-called "defensive medicine."

Entry into the medical profession is by no means unrestricted. Latest figures show, for example, that about 26,000 people took the standard medical school admissions test and only 16,000 were accepted. The number of applicants to Harvard's medical school runs to almost 3500, but the class size remains at less than 150. Some students apply to as many as 10 different medical schools and when turned down reapply two or three times. The number of students who don't apply because they know the odds are so much against them is probably two or three times the number of those who take the chance. Importantly, many applicants don't get into medical school because the number of medical schools in the United States is severely restricted.

---

[1]The demand for medical care is a relatively (although not completely) **inelastic demand** with respect to a rise in the price of medical care. That is, even a relatively large increase in the price of medical care (say, 20 percent) will cause only a modest reduction in the quantity of medical care demanded (say, 10 percent). Thus, when the relative price of medical care rises—as it has been doing for many years—consumers end up spending more on that care. Americans are spending a rising share of their incomes on medical care for another reason as well: Medical care is what economists call a **superior good**. In this context, to say that medical care is a superior good says nothing of the inherent quality of that care, good or bad. It simply means that, as their real incomes rise, consumers prefer to devote a larger share of income to medical care, just as they also spend a larger share on restaurant meals, foreign travel, and private education. In technical terms, the **income elasticity of demand** for such goods exceeds 1.

In principle, this restricted number is a result of state licensing requirements, which universally prohibit proprietary medical schools (schools run for profit). A medical school must be accredited by the state for its graduates to be allowed to take the licensing exam required for practicing medicine. And the states won't accredit schools unless the American Medical Association (AMA) certifies that the schools meet the AMA's standards. If we look back to the first decade of this century, we find that there were 192 medical schools in the United States. By 1944, that number had declined to 69. The number of physicians per 100,000 people dropped from 157 in 1900 to 132 in 1957. The reasons for these precipitous declines was the success of the AMA in controlling the output of doctors.

The regulation and certification of medical schools were based on the findings of the so-called Flexner Report. In 1910, the prestigious Carnegie Foundation commissioned Abraham Flexner[2] to inspect the existing medical education facilities in the United States. Flexner's recommendations resulted in the demise of half of the then-existing medical schools.[3] It is interesting to note than Flexner (himself not a physician or even a scientist) was examining the *inputs* and not the *outputs* of the schools. Instead of finding out how well or how qualified the *graduates* of the different schools were, he looked at how they were taught. This is equivalent to your instructor's giving you a grade on the basis of how many hours you spent studying rather than how well you did on the final exam.

The purpose of the stricture on medical schools was described by the former head of the AMA's Council on Medical Education, who said in 1928 that

[2]Flexner was a historian whose brother was the Johns Hopkins University medical dean. The model Flexner used to judge the "quality" of all other medical schools was the medical school at Johns Hopkins.

[3]Some medical historians believe that before 1900, doctors probably killed more people than they cured. The Carnegie Foundation and the AMA certainly had legitimate concerns about the quality of medical care at that time.

the reduction of the number of medical schools from 160 to 80 (resulted in) a marked reduction in number of medical students and medical graduates. We had anticipated this and felt that this was a desirable thing. We had . . . a great oversupply of poor and mediocre practitioners.

In economic terms, the supply curve shifted inward as the demand curve either remained stable or shifted outward. The result was that the price of physicians' services went up, allowing physicians to make higher incomes. The census of 1970, for example, showed that physicians had the highest income of any profession.[4] In that year, it was on average $41,500, at a time when self-employed dentists earned $28,100, engineers $17,700, and college full professors $16,800. In 1974, the median net income of physicians who incorporated themselves was $72,500. Today physicians remain the highest-paid professionals, with an average annual income of $110,000.

We can ask ourselves whether the AMA's avowed wishes were satisfied. The AMA maintained that the qualifications of many doctors were deficient—that the public was being served by doctors who were doing damage to unsuspecting patients. The idea behind medical school licensing was to weed out the most unqualified students and to eliminate the possibility of an unsuspecting sick person's being treated by an inadequately trained, yet licensed, doctor. It is strange, though, that the AMA did not seek in 1910 to analyze the qualifications of the *existing* crop of physicians. The closure of one-half of the medical schools resulted in the elimination of the *future* supply of supposedly unqualified doctors, but the supposedly unqualified doctors who were already in practice were allowed to continue practicing until retirement or death.

It is possible, too, that the *quality* of medical care consumed by the public did not increase as much as the AMA professed it did after the closure of half of the medical schools. After all, there are two kinds of medical services: One is self-

---

[4]Part of this is due, however, to longer average hours worked per week.

diagnosis and self-treatment; the other is relying on someone in the medical care industry. If the price of physician's diagnosis and treatment goes up, then one might expect the quantity demanded to fall, and an increased reliance on self-diagnosis and self-treatment would result. People would go to doctors only after their symptoms became alarming. It may be, then, that the increase in the quality—and therefore the price—of doctors' services resulted in a *decrease* in the *total* quality of medical care utilized, because doctors were consulted less often. Equivalently, when the price of the services of licensed physicians goes up, there is an increase in the demand for substitute healing services, and these substitutes may well be inferior to even a poorly trained M.D.

In addition to the AMA's restriction on the supply of physicians in the United States, there have been, at times, dramatic increases in demand, which have contributed to rising prices. Certain government programs have shifted the demand curve to the right. One of these programs is Medicare, subsidized medical care for the aged. Prior to Medicare, congressional estimates of what that program would cost were many times less than what the actual cost turned out to be. This can be easily explained, since the demand for medical services is responsive to the price charged. When Medicare was instituted, in the mid-1960s, the actual price of health care services to many older people was drastically lowered. As the price fell, the quantity demanded rose—so much so that the available supply of medical services was taxed beyond capacity. The only thing that could give was the price, and it gave. Hospital room charges and physicians' fees skyrocketed after the imposition of Medicare and its state-level counterpart for the poor, Medicaid.[5]

Similar in their effects are medical insurance plans rooted in the private sector of the economy. More than 180 million Americans are covered by some private medical insur-

---

[5]Doctors began to order just as many expensive tests for their Medicare and Medicaid patients as they did for their rich patients.

ance. Generally this insurance pays a percentage of covered medical care expenses. Herein lies a problem: Insurance usually covers more inpatient services than outpatient services. Therefore, individuals covered by insurance have an incentive to go to a hospital to be taken care of by their private doctors, and their private doctors have an incentive to send them there in order to collect payment. And, as with Medicare and Medicaid, private insurance plans increase the quantity of services demanded simply because the direct out-of-pocket costs to an insured person are very low or zero. The insurance industry has a term for this—moral hazard. In economics, we translate this term into a demand curve that slopes downward (i.e., the quantity of services demanded increases when the price falls).[6] Many medical services could be postponed or never used at all; for example, cosmetic surgery and, to a lesser extent, other elective surgery. But the lower the price charged, the more cosmetic and elective surgery will be undertaken. And the lower the price, the more likely people are to visit their doctors when they have a slight ailment, such as a cold. In other words, if people are directly charged the full price of their physicians' services, they are likely to use them more sparingly. But if the price is reduced to practically zero, some of them (at least those on the margin) will respond by seeing their physicians for minor ailments.

Furthermore, because of third-party insurance, doctors, in conjunction with hospitals, have been ordering more and more tests, using more and more advanced techniques. Hospitals have an incentive to use the most exotic techniques possible and doctors to order them, knowing full well that patients will be reimbursed by their insurance companies for a large percentage of the cost. The problem is that patients covered by insurance do not pay the *direct* cost of the medical care they receive in a hospital at the time they receive it. Obviously, they pay eventually through higher premiums, but that cost is

[6]Of course, the full price, including the insurance premium, does not fall—it rises. But the insurance premium is a fixed cost. It does not vary with the number of visits to the doctor or trips to the hospital.

spread out over everyone who buys the insurance. The result is that the quantity of services demanded in the hospital will be more than it otherwise would be. This causes hospital expenses to go up, all other things held constant.

Another reason for the high cost of medical care has been high malpractice costs, although this situation shows some sign of improving. During much of the 1970s and the first half of the 1980s, individuals sued doctors and hospitals at record rates and juries awarded larger amounts to malpractice victims each year. In 1978, an average of less than 1 doctor in 30 was sued for malpractice; in 1984, 1 doctor in 6 was sued. During the early 1980s the typical jury award in a malpractice case more than tripled, with the average award peaking at better than $1.4 million in 1986. Not surprisingly, malpractice insurance premiums skyrocketed, rising at a rate of better than 30 percent per year. In turn, health care providers passed much of these higher malpractice costs on to the consumer in the form of higher prices for health care services and more extensive testing, evaluation procedures, and consultations undertaken by physicians to prevent the possibility of lawsuit. "Defensive medicine" (procedures undertaken chiefly to reduce the risk of lawsuits) became standard practice for physicians and hospitals, costing consumers an estimated $42 billion in 1986 alone.

Recent developments suggest that some relief may be in sight. Since 1986, the average jury award has fallen by 50 percent, and fewer malpractice suits are being brought. In part these changes are due to laws passed since 1986 in 19 states, limiting the size of some types of malpractice awards and making suits more difficult to bring. Some observers also argue that jurors (themselves consumers of health care) began to realize that malpractice suits were getting out of hand. In any event, some insurers have been able to cut malpractice premiums, which should ultimately help reduce medical cost inflation.

We end this chapter with a discussion of the future supply of medical care personnel. Ironically, after decades of experiencing a shortage of doctors, the reverse is apparently soon to be the case. If current estimates are correct, by the year 1995 there will be between 70,000 and 185,000 "surplus" doctors. What has caused this turnaround in the supply of doctors? For one thing, the shortage of doctors in the past two decades and the consequent high incomes in that profession drew the maximum number to the medical field. Notwithstanding the difficulty of entering—and paying for—medical school, there has been a gradual increase in the number of graduates in the past several years. In addition, Americans going abroad for medical training and the immigration of foreign doctors have helped to increase the supply of physicians (relative to the population) from 1 doctor for every 697 Americans in 1965 to 1 doctor for every 473 Americans in 1990.

At the same time, there has been an increase in the number of alternative health care providers (such as nurse practitioners, midwives, and paramedical services) that now perform some of the functions formerly carred out only by medical doctors. Also, employers who find it hard to pay for employees' medical benefits are increasingly turning to preferred-provider organizations (PPOs) and other prepaid health plans that deliver employee medical care to employers at a lower cost. Competition from such plans seriously jeopardizes the continuing high incomes of standard fee-for-service medical practices.

Physicians who wish to pursue private practices are now facing, for the first time in decades, the problem of luring sufficient numbers of patients to their services to make a "good" living. High malpractice insurance costs, a greater supply of doctors, and the rapid development of lower-cost health care alternatives have introduced a larger element of competition into the medical profession. Although it has never been easy for a young doctor to establish a medical practice, it is now a much more difficult undertaking. Marketing seminars in selling tactics are now being taken by a number of physicians. Advertising, which became legal for the medical profession several years ago, is now more frequently resorted to by doctors, especially those just setting up a private medical practice, as are house calls, evening hours, and weekend availability. Some doctors even offer special conveniences to their patients, such as beepers for them to carry while waiting for their appointments—so they can carry on shopping or other activities until their turn comes—or TVs in waiting rooms to make delays more palatable. Obviously, the laws of supply and demand still operate, even in the medical care profession.

DISCUSSION QUESTIONS

1. The more opportunity individuals have to pass medical care costs on to third parties such as insurance companies, the less incentive they have to take care of themselves. The insurance industry calls this a problem of moral hazard. Is there any way this problem can be resolved to help reduce medical care costs?
2. Until relatively recently, doctors were not allowed to advertise their services. Even since then, some physicians have felt that the advertising of medical care services is unethical. Do you agree?

11

International Cartels

Every week, 300 of the world's richest and most prestigious diamond dealers are invited to view the "sights" in an office on Fleet Street in London. These sights are uncut diamonds being sold by the Central Selling Organization, or CSO. The CSO's nine-story office building in London is popularly known as "the syndicate." Through it every year passes 80 percent of the supply of rough-cut diamonds in the world. One organization controls that 80 percent of the supply—De-Beers, the famous diamond company. In a typical year, it markets about $2 billion worth of gems and holds an equivalent amount in its ready inventories. DeBeers also produces about 35 percent of the world's diamonds. It's clearly in a good monopoly position. The 300 diamond dealers who come in every week are shown the diamonds and told the price. Haggling is essentially not allowed; in fact, it is rumored that if one haggles, one is not asked back.

If DeBeers were simply the producer of 35 percent of the world's diamonds, it might not have such an effective control on the market price of diamonds; but it has been successful in forming a very strong cartel-type arrangement in which it is the sole marketing agent of another 45 percent of the world's rough-cut diamonds. In this way it becomes an effective monopoly: It controls the sales, or more specifically the amount of sales, that are offered to diamond dealers throughout the world. It can do what a monopolist wishes to do—restrict output and thereby raise the price above what it would be in a perfectly competitive situation.

Another successful international cartel is OPEC, the Organization of Petroleum Exporting Countries. In 1960, OPEC started as an organization designed to assist the oil-exporting countries. By 1970 it included Abu Dhabi, Algeria, Indonesia, Iran, Iraq, Kuwait, Libya, Nigeria, Qatar, Saudi Arabia, and Venezuela; since then a few other countries, including Ecuador, have joined the group, and other nations have left the cartel. During the 1960s, OPEC's success was limited because an ever-expanding world supply of oil kept prices down. Even though demand was growing, new discoveries expanded the supplies so fast that nominal well-head prices for crude oil actually fell slightly between 1960 and 1970. Then in 1970, Libya, which had become a major supplier of crude oil to Western European markets, had a revolution. The new regime cut output sharply in a partly political move against the oil companies to which concessions had been granted by the previous regime. Libya's cutback made sizable price increases possible in 1971. These increases were ratified by the other members of OPEC in agreements drawn up in Tripoli and Teheran. Much of the success of this rise in prices was credited to OPEC, although some observers contended that Libya was alone responsible and had no help from OPEC.

The main ingredient in OPEC's success, however, was the outbreak of war in the Middle East in 1973. In the wake of this war, Saudi Arabia, Kuwait, and a few smaller Arab countries agreed to cut back greatly their production of crude oil, thus paving the way for large price increases. Remember that the only way to raise prices when one is a monopolist is to cut back on production and sales. Thus, OPEC members could have an effective cartel arrangement only if some or all of them cut back on production and sales. Since Saudi Arabia, which accounts for the bulk of the oil production in the Middle East, did cut back greatly in 1973, the cartel arrangement worked, and it continued to work for several years. The total profits for the oil-exporting countries were increased greatly as a result.

The effect of OPEC cartelization activities on world oil prices was dramatic. On January 1, 1973, one could buy Saudi Arabian crude oil at $2.12 a barrel. Within one year, the price of crude had risen to $7.61 per barrel; by 1975, to $10.50; and by the end of the decade, the nominal price of oil was *ten times* what it had been just seven years before.

Other international cartels have been formed, many of them involved with internationally traded commodities. The International Bauxite Association (IBA) has attempted to control the price of bauxite around the world. The International Tin Agreement has existed since before World War II. The Organization of Banana-Exporting Countries has tried to duplicate OPEC's success. There are producer cartels in iron ore, mercury, tea, tropical timber, natural rubber, nickel, cobalt, tungsten, columbium, pepper, tantalum, and quinine, and probably many more. Not all of them are successful. We now ask the question: What are the necessary ingredients to a successful cartel arrangement?

A cartel must meet four basic requirements if it is to be successful:

1. It must control a large share of total actual and potential output. It must not face substantial competition from outsiders.
2. Available substitutes must be limited. In other words, the price elasticity of demand for the product in question must be fairly low; that is, there must be a relatively inelastic demand.
3. The demand for the cartel's product must be relatively stable, regardless of business conditions. If this is not

the case, then the amount sold at any given price will be greater during economic **expansions** than during **recessions**, and the cartel will find it difficult to maintain any given price and output combination for very long.

4. Producers must be willing and able to withhold sufficient amounts of their product to affect the market. Each member must resist the temptation to cheat. And consumers must not be able to have large stockpiles of the product on which to draw.

There are probably other conditions that would make a cartel's success probability even greater, but these can be considered the basic ones.

A big cause of cartel instability is cheating. When there are many firms or countries in a cartel arrangement, there will always be some that are unhappy with the situation. They will want to cheat by charging a slightly lower price than the one stipulated by the cartel. Members who are producing a small percentage of the total output of the cartel essentially face a very elastic demand curve if they cheat and no one else does. A small drop in price by a cheater will result in a very large increase in total revenues.

There will always be cartel members who figure that it will pay them to cut prices. Each firm will try to do this, thinking that the others will not do the same thing. Or a firm may decide that other firms are going to cheat anyway, so why shouldn't it be the first? Obviously, though, when a sufficient number of firms in the cartel try to cheat, the cartel breaks up. We would expect, therefore, that as long as the cartel is not-maintained by force of law, there will be a constant threat to its existence. Its members will have a large incentive to cut prices; and once a couple of members do that, the rest may follow.

Consider, for example, the failure of the copper cartel, CIPEC, the Intergovernmental Council of Copper Exporting Countries. CIPEC was founded in 1967 by Chile, Zambia, Zaire, and Peru. It still exists, but it has never managed to show any muscle in world markets. In 1974 the price of copper started falling. From April to the end of December, it had dropped by 55 percent. CIPEC was powerless to bring it back up. Why? Because most of the developing countries are unwilling or unable to limit their output of copper. There isn't a Saudi Arabia of the copper world that is willing to cut back 50 percent on production so that the rest of the cartel can enjoy higher prices. Remember, the only way to keep prices up is to keep production down.

The coffee cartel hasn't fared much better. The price of coffee has gone up and down like a yoyo. Every time the price starts falling, big coffee producers such as Colombia and Brazil urge other producing nations to cut back. They do so at the annual meeting of the Council of International Coffee Organization (ICO). Moreover, ICO has found out what the price elasticity of demand for coffee really is. Each time the price has jumped, the quantity demanded has fallen, sometimes dramatically. Several years ago, for example, the general manager of Colombia's coffee growers' federation thought that the 60-cent-per-pound increase in the average retail price during the previous two years had caused consumption to drop by 15 percent. His suggestion to other coffee producers at that time? Lower prices. In other words, even a strong cartel cannot face up to the possibility of consumers cutting back on the consumption of a higher-priced good.

Cartel instability, or lack of success, is not confined to business firms or even to nations engaging in international commodities selling. Have you ever noticed how short-lived a homemakers' boycott of a supermarket is? There are so many members in that particular cartel that it is difficult for one of them not to "cheat" and actually go out and buy some food from the supermarket. It is impossible to police the large number of homemakers involved.

Consider one more example, which is hypothetical. If you are in a class of 100 students whose exams will be graded on a curve, how easily could all of you get together and agree to cut down study time? Would your cartel be successful? The answer, of course, depends on each individual student's incentive to cheat on the cartel by studying more. If only one student were to study longer than all the others, that student would get a higher grade than he or she would otherwise have received. If enough students do this, the cartel will break down and everyone will end up where they started: competing.

A variety of market forces, including the incentive to cheat, have proved capable of battering even the most successful cartels. Consider, for example, the DeBeers-led CSO diamond cartel. In 1980, the wholesale price of investment-grade D-Flawless diamonds—considered the most reliable measure of market conditions in the industry—was about $55,000 per carat. A worldwide recession starting in 1981 caused a decline in the demand for all goods, particularly long-lived assets such as diamonds. The recession also sharply cut inflation, further reducing the demand for collectibles and so-called "hard" assets as individuals, particularly in the United States, no longer sought inflation hedges. Despite DeBeers' best efforts to reduce the amount of diamonds supplied to the market, prices of the gems dropped sharply. Downward pressure on prices was intensified by Australia's huge new Ashton mine, which began full-scale production in 1986 and which may have added as much as 40 percent to world diamond production. By 1987, the price of D-Flawless gems was languishing between $14,000 and $17,000 per carat. Although economic expansion helped boost diamond prices over the next few years, the nominal price of investment-grade diamonds in 1990 was still better than 60 percent below the peak levels of 1980. Indeed, after adjusting for the general rise in the price level, D-Flawless diamonds are now worth only about 25 cents on the dollar compared to 1980.

The OPEC oil cartel has also been unsuccessful in holding the line on prices. The years of relatively high oil prices, which began with the "energy crisis" of 1973, brought forth substantial increases in the worldwide supply of petroleum. Combined with the recession that began in 1981, the new supplies put enormous competitive pressure on the oil cartel; in March of 1983, for the first time in its 23-year history, OPEC agreed to cut the posted prices of its crude oil. War between the oil-producing nations of Iran and Iraq added to OPEC's woes, as those two nations cheated on their output quotas, increasing production to help finance heavy military expenditures. By 1986, oil prices were in "free fall." The price of crude oil, which had been $35 per barrel in late 1980 and early 1981, dropped to but $10 a barrel in 1986, as cheating on output quotas spread throughout the cartel. OPEC member Saudi Arabia, the world's largest producer of crude, finally managed to restore order, as it threatened to double its output if other OPEC members didn't begin adhering to quotas. By the end of the decade, crude prices were hovering in the range of $18–20 per barrel; in terms of inflation-adjusted dollars, prices had fallen by two-thirds since 1980. Although OPEC has been among the most successful of all cartels on record, it too has found that, ultimately, market forces exert powerful control over those who seek to suppress competition.

DISCUSSION QUESTIONS

1. Why are all cartels inherently unstable?
2. Would it be easier to form a cartel in a market with many producers or one with very few producers?

12

Bailout at $300 Billion: The Great S&L Mess

When President George Bush gave final approval to the Financial Institutions Reform, Recovery, and Enforcement Act of 1989, the Congressional leaders attending the signing ceremony burst into applause. Bush's signature on the legislation made it official that the "full faith and credit" of the United States government would now guarantee the financial obligations of the nation's savings and loan (S&L) industry. Since those obligations include liabilities of ailing S&Ls that are expected ultimately to exceed the S&Ls' assets by some *$300 billion*, it is little wonder that the event made headlines throughout the country. What is perhaps more surprising is the lack of attention paid to one simple fact: The full faith and credit of the government ultimately rests on the ability of the taxpayers to foot the bill. Thus, by the simple act of putting pen to paper, the president who campaigned for office on a platform of "no new taxes" had committed American taxpayers to $300 billion in new taxes—and was applauded for doing so.

To understand why the average American family will get stuck with a bill for $4800 to pay off the bad debts of the nation's savings and loans, we must go back 60 years, to the time of the Great Depression. Between 1929 and 1933 the American economy went into a tailspin of unprecedented magnitude. National income fell by 50 percent and unemployment rose to 25 percent. Tens of thousands of farms and businesses went out of existence; and when they did so, their financial obligations to banks and other lenders became uncollectible. As a consequence, many banks and other savings institutions suffered substantial financial losses. When those losses became known to the public, depositors lost faith in the banking industry, and many sought to close out their checking and savings accounts, feeling that cash was far safer. The resulting series of "bank runs" forced many banks to close their doors, which further eroded public confidence in our country's financial institutions. Ultimately, the federal government stepped in, establishing the Federal Deposit Insurance Corporation (FDIC), a government corporation that guaranteed bank deposits up to $5000. Shortly thereafter, the Federal Savings and Loan Insurance Corporation (FSLIC) was formed, a separate government corporation offering a similar guarantee for deposits of the nation's savings and loans (S&Ls). These government guarantees were sufficient to restore the public's confidence in the country's financial system, and the bank runs that had brought the country to the brink of financial collapse quickly ceased.

Both the FDIC and the FSLIC were originally self-financed, using insurance premiums on deposits held by member banks and S&Ls to cover the costs of paying off depositors of banks or S&Ls that failed. Not surprisingly, since the FDIC and the FSLIC were guaranteeing bank and S&L deposits, they felt it appropriate to impose rules upon the borrowing and lending behavior of those institutions. These rules covered accounting procedures, the types of assets that banks and S&Ls could own, and the liabilities they could incur. Additional regulations controlled the interest rates that banks and S&Ls could pay their depositors. Over time, the size of deposits insured by the FDIC and the FSLIC was raised to $40,000 per account, but the government regulations prohibiting high-risk investments by banks and S&Ls ensured that the deposit-insurance premiums were sufficient to cover the occasional losses incurred by institutions that failed.

By the late 1970s, many people in the financial community felt that the layers of regulations imposed by the FDIC and the FSLIC had become excessive. Banks and S&Ls, it was said, could no longer compete effectively in a rapidly changing financial environment. As a result, in 1980 the law was changed to give banks and savings and loans greater freedom in the interest rates they paid depositors, and more latitude in the assets and liabilities they held. In addition, the maximum deposit guaranteed by the government was raised to $100,000. In effect, the loosened regulations gave banks and S&Ls the freedom to hold riskier assets and liabilities; the lifting of interest rate controls gave them the ability to attract those assets (chiefly deposits) and thus create those liabilities (mostly loans); and the hike in the size of the maximum insured deposit allowed them to shift more of the risk to the government (i.e., the taxpayer). The banking and S&L industries responded rapidly to the new freedom and incentives, competing vigorously for new deposits by offering record-high interest rates, and seeking new ways of investing their depositors' money. As it turned out, S&Ls were the most aggressive in pursuing their new-found freedom, and it is in that industry where the adverse effects of deregulation have been most prominent.[1]

---

[1]Although we focus here on the problems associated with S&Ls, many of the incentives facing them also face commercial banks. Thus, some observers are predicting that the problems encountered by S&Ls will, at least to some degree, also plague banks.

When the S&L industry was deregulated in 1980, the prices of Midwest farmland and Southwest oil properties were escalating rapidly, even relative to the overall rate of inflation, making loans for the purchase of such properties look like a "sure bet" to the owners of many S&Ls. As it turned out, the early 1980s were a lot less prosperous than many people—especially the owners of S&Ls—had expected. Less than a year after deregulation, the recession of 1981–82, one of the most severe on record, sent unemployment soaring and land prices plunging. Declining oil prices and drought further depressed land prices in the Southwest and Midwest. Since S&Ls make most of their loans to people who are purchasing real estate, the **collateral** backing those loans drastically shrank in value. In many cases, the value of the collateral fell below the face value of the loans—encouraging borrowers to simply default on their loans, and leaving the S&Ls with huge losses when they had to sell the property in depressed real estate markets.

The industry's losses were compounded by another problem: High-flying entrepreneurs, many of them real estate developers in states such as Texas, Florida, and California, got into the savings and loan industry around 1982. Strapped for cash in a time of record-high interest rates, and viewing S&Ls as a cheap source of funds, they purchased them at a record pace. Then they began to use them. At best, the new owners pumped government-insured funds into doomed real estate development projects. At worst—well, some have called it theft.

The size of the problem began to emerge in 1986, with numerous savings and loans reporting huge losses. By 1988, nearly 400 S&Ls (out of 3300 in existence) were considered to be in such bad financial condition that the FSLIC would have to step in and bail them out. More than half of these had gotten into trouble making risky loans. And, regulators say, outright fraud contributed to the failure of at least 50. The liabilities of the "zombies" (as they are termed)—dead but still walking—totaled more than $125 billion, exposing the FSLIC to huge potential losses. During a six-month period spanning the end of 1987 and the beginning of 1988, S&Ls lost nearly $8 billion. By the summer of 1989, they were losing that much each *month*. Overall, the failure rate for S&Ls in the 1980s was higher than it was during the Great Depression.

Although declining land prices, fraud, and high interest rates contributed to the woes of the S&Ls, the root of the problem lies in the incentives created by the deposit insurance system. Imagine taking $100,000 worth of someone else's money to Las Vegas and having a government agency make you the following deal: For a small insurance premium (specifically, $87.50), you can gamble all you want; if you lose money, the government will reimburse you fully; if you win, you get to keep the winnings (less a small interest payment to the person who lent you the $100,000). Not surprisingly, you would probably head for the riskiest game in the house—which is just what the nation's S&Ls did in the 1980s.

Prior to 1980, tight government regulations largely precluded S&Ls from making speculative, high-risk loans; hence, S&L funds went chiefly toward financing home mortgages. When regulations were eased, many S&Ls responded exactly as would be predicted: They went looking for the riskiest game in town. On average, risky loans and investments can only compete with safer investments by offering the promise of higher average returns. But the very nature of risky projects means that they sometimes end up losing money. When lenders or investors are risking their own funds, they are careful to weigh the higher average returns of risky investments against the greater chance that such investments will lose money. But the S&Ls were fundamentally playing with someone else's money—the taxpayers'. They knew that if they lost money on their loans and investments, they could ultimately get the government (i.e., taxpayers) to foot the bill. Thus, once freed from the heavy hand of regulation, they made loans for speculative oil drilling and land deals, questionable shopping center developments, and just about any other project that offered the chance of potentially high returns—but also carried a big chance of failure. In many cases, the S&Ls did not require borrowers to put up any of their own money, and sometimes they even lent enough funds to cover interest payments for the first year or two. Eventually, the questionable lending practices of the S&Ls caught up with them, and they began to lose money at record rates.

Some of the worst S&Ls were closed by the FSLIC as early as 1984, but it took a good bit longer for the regulators to catch up with most of them. The industry's daily losses of $6 million to $10 million—which the FSLIC could, just barely, cover out of insurance premiums—quickly mounted to daily losses of $60 million to $100 million. It soon became clear that the problem had gone far beyond the resources of FSLIC, and that more drastic action was in order.

Thus came the enactment of the Financial Institutions Reform, Recovery and Enforcement Act of 1989. On the institutional side, the law abolished the Federal Home Loan Bank Board, which had been in charge of writing and enforcing S&L regulations. In its place is the newly formed Office of Thrift Supervision, a division of the U.S. Treasury Department, which was given expanded regulatory powers over the S&Ls. To clean up the existing financial mess in the industry, the act established the Resolution Trust Corporation (RTC), which is empowered to sell off the assets of failed S&Ls, close down the remaining zombies, and borrow enough money to pay off existing and anticipated future net liabilities of the industry.

Financially, the big-ticket item in the act is the RTC's budget. First-year expenditures of the RTC are estimated to be *at least* $50 billion, and the agency's spending over the next 20 years will total $300 billion or more—some $1200 for each man, woman, and child in the United States. All of this spending ultimately will be paid for by the American taxpayer, and all of it will go to just one purpose—paying off the bad debts accumulated by the savings and loan industry during the 1980s.[2]

---

[2]The costs to society of the mistakes and, possibly, fraud committed by S&Ls during the 1980s have, of course, already been incurred. The 1989 legislation simply decrees the extent to which those costs will be borne by taxpayers rather than by S&L owners and depositors.

Although the federal government has participated in commercial "bailouts" in the past—most notably involving the Chrysler Corp. and aerospace giant Lockheed Corp., the combined scope and nature of the S&L bailout is unprecedented. First, the S&L bailout is more than 100 times larger than anything seen before. Second, the assistance of the government is not in the form of loans and loan guarantees, as in the past; instead, the government is actually taking over the obligations of the ailing S&Ls and paying them off. The owners of the S&Ls are simply free to walk away from the mess they have created, leaving taxpayers with the bill.

Despite the enormous expected cost of the S&L bailout plan, most observers doubt the legislation will get the job done and, in any event, is likely to cost much more than the government is willing to admit. First, the bill's cost estimates are based on an economic outlook for the future that is, even in the eyes of government officials, "optimistic." Even a moderate recession during the 1990s could hike the bill's costs by 10 percent, and a severe recession similar to the one in 1981–82 could drive up costs by 20 percent or more.

Second, the schedule for closing sick S&Ls appears grossly inadequate. Plans for the first year of operation called for the RTC to deal with the obligations of 400 S&Ls. Yet at the time of the bill's passage, 264 thrifts were *already* in government hands, and the administrator of the Office of Thrift Supervision was quietly admitting that the RTC might be confronted with the bad debts of 50 percent more S&Ls than allowed for in its budget. "Woefully inadequate" is the term used by one observer to describe the government's proposed budget for the bailout; another called the plan "a fantasy."

Finally, there are doubts that the new legislation will prevent a recurrence of the problem. It's true that the bill requires S&L owners to put more of their own assets at risk, in the form of new "capital requirements" for S&Ls. Nevertheless, the new requirements only amount to 3 percent of deposits, leaving the other 97 percent a potential liability for taxpayers. Savings and loan deposits will continue to be insured against losses, and there is little assurance that government officials have learned how to prevent S&L abuses without regulating the industry out of existence. Many commentators seem to agree with the president of a major S&L trade association, who said, "It's only a matter of time before we revisit this issue." Another observer was even more explicit, arguing, "There inevitably will be plans called Bush II, Bush III, and Bush IV." If a sequel to the 1989 legislation is indeed a sure thing, perhaps President Bush should have chosen a more auspicious date for the signing ceremony—say, Halloween, or even Friday the 13th.

DISCUSSION QUESTIONS

1. Why do you think the government insures depositors at banks and savings and loans against financial losses, but generally does not insure the owners of corporate stocks and bonds against financial losses?
2. How do you think the behavior of the local pizza parlor might be different if the government insured the owner against losing any money?

Part Three

Factor Markets

INTRODUCTION

Supply and demand analysis also applies to the market for factors of production. These factors of production may be in the form of **labor** or **capital**. Most of the chapters in this part deal with the factor we call *labor*. Chapter 13, which examines the effect of divorce on the labor-market opportunities for women, illustrates once again how economics can be applied to what seem to be fundamentally noneconomic issues. The impact of taxation on labor-market choices forms the principle focus of Chapters 14 and 17, although Chapter 14 also reveals that a seemingly isolated episode—the post–World War II "baby boom"—can continue to have important ramifications for years (indeed, decades).

Chapter 15 examines the impact of rent control, revealing the pervasive and ofttimes perverse consequences when governments attempt to interfere with market exchanges: Rent controls, imposed in the hope of making housing more affordable, typically make housing *less* affordable for many, and unattainable at all for some. In Chapter 16, we take a broad look at the multiple factors of production, as we view police decision making as an attempt to minimize the cost of producing any given level of police output (crime prevention).

Again, we remind the reader that we are not analyzing individuals' thought processes, but rather their observed behavior patterns and the way those behavior patterns change according to changing constraints. Just as Sir Isaac Newton's fabled apple did not need to understand gravity in order to land on Sir Isaac's head, market participants need not understand the principles of our analysis in order to behave in a manner consistent with our predictions.

13

Women and Divorce

Today, almost 7 million women are making more income than their mates. And another 3 million women are earning at least 80 percent of the pay of their husbands.

What kind of women outstrip their husbands in earning capacity? The Census Bureau reports that wives with higher wages are most likely to be working full time, year round, with no minor children at home. Also, they usually have completed college and are employed in a professional, administrative, executive, or managerial occupation.

What does the fact that some women are making almost as much as, or more than, their husbands have to do with the title of this chapter? As it turns out, economic theory predicts that divorce rates will be influenced by, among other things,

TABLE 13-1   Percentage of Men and Women Ever Married Who Were Known to Have Been Divorced, by Place of Residence

	Divorce Rates	
Location	Male	Female
Urban	14.6%	15.5%
Rural nonfarm	13.1	12.0
Farm	7.4	6.6

the earning capacity of women. In the most general sense, the more that a married woman can earn on her own, the less she has to give up if she chooses to become divorced. In other words, the opportunity cost of divorce is lower for women with higher earning potential.

We can apply this theory to information gleaned about divorce rates of rural versus urban females. Look at Table 13-1. As you can see, farm men and women have substantially lower divorce rates than either rural nonfarm (small-town) men and women or urban men and women. A sociological or psychological explanation of these data might be that life is happier for men and women on the farm than it is for urban couples. It is indeed possible that this is true. Economists, however, look for explanations based on the choices available to individuals and the relative costs and benefits attached to these choices. That is to say, when looking for explanations of real-world phenomena, economists will tend to look at opportunity costs and trade-offs and interpret events in these terms.

Department of Labor statistics tell us that about 55 percent of nonfarm women are in the labor force, but only about 35 percent of farm women are employed (off the farm). In other words, farm women tend to specialize more in household and on-farm work, relative to nonfarm women. Men, on farms and off, tend to specialize in nonhousehold work. This implies that the bundles of skills possessed by husband and wife are more likely to be different on farms than off farms. The gains to marriage are therefore greater in a farming household, on average, than in a nonfarming household. Essentially, then, we would predict that farm households would be more stable than nonfarm households. Moreover, we would predict that the opportunity cost of remaining married for the farm wife who has specialized in household and on-farm work would be lower than the opportunity cost of a nonfarm wife who is employed in a nonfarm job. Equivalently, the nonfarm wife will give up less by becoming divorced, because she already has an earning capacity.

Take another look at Table 13-1. You will note that the divorce rate for women living on farms is lower than for men living on farms. But the *opposite* is true in urban areas, where females have a higher divorce rate than males. How can we explain this? Economic theory assumes that individuals desire to maximize their net benefits, and that in order to do so, they will seek out their best opportunities. That is to say, they will tend to migrate to wherever the best opportunities exist. When a farm marriage ends in divorce, the male typically retains farm ownership; he stays on the farm to work. The female, on the other hand, moves to where her job opportunities will be greater—to urban areas. In effect, divorced women migrate from the farm to the city, while divorced men do not.

Census data also reveal that divorce rates for farm women are higher among women who live on farms located in areas with relatively dense populations, such as Massachusetts and New Jersey. Can economic theory also help us understand why this would be the case? As it turns out, yes. Farm women living in those areas, because of their closer proximity to urban labor markets, have a better knowledge of other labor opportunities. That means that in those areas the opportunity cost to women on farms of learning about alternative uses of their labor is less. Also, in such relatively densely populated areas it is much easier to work at nonfarm jobs—which means, among other things, that they have less incentive to invest in farm-specific skills only. By contrast, farm women living in the sparsely populated states of Nevada and Wyoming, for example, have not had similar opportunities to become aware of job alternatives off the farm, or to learn nonfarm-specific skills. Therefore, they have tended to specialize more in farm-specific skills and household skills. We would predict, therefore, that the differences between farm and nonfarm divorce rates is lowest in the most densely populated states and highest in the most sparsely populated states. Indeed, the data show that this prediction is accurate.

Increasing numbers of nonfarm women are entering the work force each year. As the number of farms shrinks each year, many farm women, along with their families, are being forced to leave the business of farming and also are entering the nonfarm labor market. And, slowly but surely, wages for women are rising relative to wages of men. Does this mean that the divorce rate will increase in the future? If the assumptions in this chapter are correct, then we can predict that it will. In general, the greater the number of opportunities available to an individual, and the lower the cost of those opportunities, the more likely it is that they will be explored—and sometimes this entails a divorce.

DISCUSSION QUESTIONS

1. On the basis of the analysis given in this chapter, would you expect divorce rates to be highest among women who have the highest incomes?
2. To what extent do you think opportunities and opportunity costs are determining factors in other family decisions, such as childbearing and educational choices?

14

The Graying of America

America is aging. The baby boomers who pushed the Beatles and the Rolling Stones into stardom are entering middle age. Indeed, the future of America is now on display in Florida, where nearly one person in five is over 65. In 30 years, almost 20 percent of *all* Americans will be 65 or older. Just as the post–World War II baby boom presented both obstacles and opportunities, so too does the graying of America. Let's see why.

Two principal forces are behind America's "senior boom." First, we're living longer. Average life expectancy in 1900 was 47. Today it is 75, and is likely to reach 80 within a decade. Second, the birth rate is plummeting. Today's mothers are having *half* the number of children that their mothers had. In short, the old are living longer and the ranks of the young are shrinking. Together, these forces are pushing up the proportion of the population over 65. In 1970, the **median age** in the United States—the age that divides the older half of the population from the younger half—was 28; today the median age is 33, and is rising rapidly. Compounding these factors, the average age at retirement has been declining as well— from 65 in 1963 to 62 currently. The result is more retirees relying on fewer workers to help ensure that their senior years are also golden years.

Why should a person who is, say, college age be concerned with age of the rest of the population? Well, old people are expensive. In fact, people over 65 now consume a bit over one-third of the federal government's budget. Social Security payments to retirees are the biggest item, now running about $240 billion a year. Medicare, which pays hospital and doctors' bills for the elderly, costs over $100 billion a year and is swelling in size by 10 percent annually. Moreover, fully a third of the $60-billion-a-year budget for Medicaid, which helps pay medical bills for the poor of all ages, goes to those over the age of 65.

Under current law, the elderly will consume nearly 40 percent of all federal spending within 20 years. By 2010, Medicare *alone* will cost more than national defense, and the number of "very old"—people over 85, and most in need of care— will have doubled to six million. Within 40 years, nearly *one-half* of the federal budget will go to the old. In a nutshell, senior citizens are the beneficiaries of an expensive and rapidly growing share of all federal spending. What are they getting for our dollars?

To begin with, the elderly are already more prosperous than ever. In 1990 dollars, the annual discretionary income of those over 65 averages about $7400 per capita. That's 30 percent *higher* than the average discretionary income of all age groups. Each year, inflation-adjusted Social Security benefits paid new retirees are higher than the first-year benefits paid people who retired the year before. And for the past 20 years, cost-of-living adjustments have protected Social Security benefits from inflation. The impact of Social Security is evident even at the lower end of the income scale: The poverty rate for people over 65 is *lower* than for the population as a whole. Retired people today collect Social Security benefits that are two to five *times* what they and their employers contributed in payroll taxes, plus interest earned.

Not surprisingly, medical expenses are a major concern for many elderly. Perhaps reflecting that concern, every man, woman, and child in America currently pays almost $500 *per year* in federal taxes to subsidize medical care for the elderly. Indeed, no other country in the world goes to the lengths that America does to preserve life. Almost 30 percent of Medicare's budget goes to patients in their last year of life. Coronary by-pass operations—costing $25,000 apiece—are routinely performed on Americans in their 60s and even 70s. And for those over 65, Medicare picks up the tab. Even heart transplants are now performed on people in their 60s—and paid for by Medicare for those over 65. By contrast, the Japanese offer no organ transplants. Britain's National Health Service generally will not provide kidney dialysis for people over 55. Yet Medicare subsidizes dialysis for more than 100,000 people, half of them over 60. The cost: more than $2 billion a year. Overall, the elderly receive Medicare benefits worth five to twenty *times* the payroll taxes (plus interest) they paid for this program.

The responsibility for the enormous—and growing—bills for Social Security and Medicare falls squarely on current and future workers, because both programs are financed by taxes on payrolls. Twenty years ago, these programs were adequately financed with a payroll levy of less than 10 percent of the typical worker's earnings. Today, the tax rate exceeds 15 percent of median wages, and is expected to grow rapidly.

By the year 2020, early baby boomers, born in the late 1940s and early 1950s will have retired. Late baby boomers, born in the 1960s, will be nearing retirement. Both groups will leave today's college students—and their children—with a staggering bill to pay. For Social Security and Medicare to stay as they are, the payroll tax rate may have to rise to 25 percent of wages over the next 30 years. And a payroll tax rate of 40 percent is not unlikely by the middle of the twenty-first century.

One way to think of the enormous bill facing today's college students—and their successors—is to consider the number of retirees each worker must support. In 1946, the burden of one Social Security recipient was shared by 42 workers. By 1960, nine workers had to foot the bill for each retiree's Social Security benefits. Today, roughly three workers pick up the tab for each retiree's Social Security, *plus* his or her Medicare benefits. By 2030, only two workers will be available to pay the Social Security and Medicare benefits due each recipient. Thus a working couple will have to support not only itself and its family, but also someone outside the family who is receiving Social Security and Medicare benefits.

Paying all the bills presented by the twenty-first century's senior citizens will be made more difficult by another fact: Older workers are leaving the workplace in record numbers. We noted earlier that the average retirement age is down to 62 and declining. Only 32 percent of the people age 55 and over hold jobs today, compared with 45 percent in 1930. Thus, even as the elderly are making increasing demands on the federal budget, fewer of them are staying around to help foot the bill.

Part of the exodus of the old from the workplace is due simply to their prosperity. Older people have higher disposable incomes than any other age group in the population—and are using it to consume more leisure. Importantly, however, the changing work habits of older individuals have been prompted—perhaps inadvertently—by American businesses. As Daniel Knowles, vice president of Grumman Corp., put it: "Young people don't discriminate against old people. Old people do. Young people aren't in positions of power." According to James Rosenbaum, a Northwestern University professor, such discrimination is one reason career advancement often slows after age 40. Perhaps because they have trouble imagining an *old* "go-getter," 62 percent of

American corporations offer early retirement plans, while only 4 percent offer inducements to delay retirement. Looking ahead to career dead ends and hefty retirement checks, increasing numbers of older workers are opting for the golf course instead of the morning commute.

Even more important than the attitudes and policies of businesses, however, may be the federal government's tax treatment of the elderly. Much ado has made about cuts in **marginal tax rates** in recent years, and some elderly have indeed benefited from lower income tax rates. Yet tax reform has done little about the other taxes seniors face. Individuals age 65 and over, especially those in middle-income brackets, can be subject to a crushing array of taxes. Among other levies they must pay are taxes on up to one-half of their Social Security benefits; payroll taxes if they keep working; the loss of $1 in Social Security benefits for every $2 of wage income over $8880; and even taxes on supposedly "tax-exempt" municipal bonds. Because these taxes can "piggyback" on each other, effective marginal tax rates can become truly astronomical for the elderly. In fact, for a fairly typical couple trying to supplement their retirement checks, income from work can be subject to a tax rate in excess of *80%*—turning a $5-per-hour part-time job into a $1-per-hour pittance. It's little wonder that so many seniors are saying "no thanks" to seemingly attractive jobs.

So far, only the private sector has begun to realize that the graying of America requires that we rethink the role of senior citizens in the work force. And some firms are doing more than just thinking. Builders Emporium, for example, a major chain of home centers in California, has begun vigorously recruiting senior citizens as sales clerks. The result has been a sharp increase in customer satisfaction: The older workers know the merchandise better and have more experience in dealing with people. Moreover, turnover and absenteeism have plummeted. People with gray hair, it seems, are immune to "surfer's throat," a malady that strikes younger Californians before sunny weekends.

Other firms have introduced "retirement transition programs." Instead of early retirement at age 55 or 60, for example, older workers are encouraged to simply cut back on their workweek while staying on the job. Often, it is possible for workers to get the best of both worlds, collecting a retirement check even while working part-time at the same firm. Another strategy recognizes the importance of rewarding superior performance among older workers. At some firms, for example, senior technical managers are relieved of the drudgery of mundane management tasks, and allowed to spend more time focusing on the technical side of their specialties. To sweeten the pot, a pay hike is often included in the package.

Apparently, programs such as these are beginning to pay off. In one recent survey, more than 70 percent of the 400 businesses queried gave their older workers top marks for job performance; over 80 percent of the seniors received ratings of excellent or very good for their commitment to quality. Moreover, many firms are finding that the retention of older workers cuts training and pension costs sharply and, because older workers are less likely to have school-age children, even reduces health insurance outlays.

Congress thus far seems oblivious to the pitfalls and promises of an aging America. Indeed, in 1988 Congress passed an expensive "catastrophic care" extension of Medicare, to be financed with a hefty **surtax** on the workplace earnings of senior citizens. The program was billed as benefiting the elderly, but the supposed beneficiaries immediately recognized the plan as offering high costs but scant benefits. The result was a veritable firestorm of complaints by senior citizens, which forced a severely singed Congress to repeal the plan in 1989.

If Social Security and Medicare are kept on their current paths, and older workers continue to be taxed out of the work force, the future burden on those who are today's college students is likely to be unbearable. If we are to avoid the social tension and enormous costs of such an outcome, the willingness and ability of older individuals to retain more of their self-sufficiency must be recognized. To do otherwise is to invite a future in which the golden years are but memories of the past.

DISCUSSION QUESTIONS

1. How do the payroll taxes levied on the earnings of workers affect their decisions about how much leisure they consume?
2. When the government taxes younger people so as to pay benefits to older people, how does this affect the amount of assistance that younger people might *voluntarily* choose to offer older people?

15

Bankrupt Landlords, from Sea to Shining Sea

Lena Schunk is 91 years old and her health is not what it used to be. Currently, she lives on the top floor of her two-story house in the city of Santa Monica, a beachfront enclave of Los Angeles. Unable to negotiate the stairs, she would like to move to the first floor of her house. She can't, however, because the young woman renting the first-floor apartment from Schunk refuses to move out. Sound strange? Not in Santa Monica—known locally as the People's Republic of Santa Monica—where stringent rent control laws prevent Mrs. Schunk from evicting her downstairs tenant.

Three thousand miles to the east, rent control laws in New York City—known locally as the Big Apple—are forcing landlords to *abandon* 2000 housing units a *month* because the owners no longer can afford the financial losses imposed by rent control. Largely as a result of such abandonments, the city government of New York now owns more than 150,000 derelict housing units—empty, save for rats and small-time cocaine dealers. Meanwhile, because the controls also discourage new construction, the city faces a "housing gap" of 184,000 rental units—apartments that easily could be filled at current controlled rental rates, *if* the units existed in habitable form.

From coast to coast, stories like these are commonplace in the 200-plus American cities and towns that practice some form of rent control—a system in which the local government tells building owners how much they can charge for rent. Time and again, the stories are the same: poorly maintained rental units; abandoned apartment buildings; tenants trapped by housing gridlock in apartments no longer suitable for them; bureaucracies bloated with rent control enforcers; and even homeless families that can find *no one* who will rent to them. And time and again, the reason for the stories is the same: legal limits on the rent that people may pay for a place to live.

To help in understanding the pervasive consequences of rent control, it will be useful to describe briefly the way a market adjusts to changes in supply and demand, in both the short run and the long run. By the short run, we mean a period of time too brief for the construction of new housing units. Note that this does *not* mean that the supply of housing is completely inelastic. Even though the *physical* stock of housing is fixed, a higher price for housing will yield a larger *effective* amount of housing: Higher prices encourage people who own homes or housing units to conserve on their own usage of them—as, for example, Mrs. Schunk did when she originally rented out part of her Santa Monica home. Thus, even in the short run, the elasticity of supply is positive. As a consequence, an increase in demand reflecting an increase in people seeking apartments—such as occurred in New York during World War II and in Santa Monica during the 1970s—typically

leads to a sharp increase in rental prices and a resulting increase in the effective quantity of units available.

In the long run, the market system yields forces that
make for a new equilibrium. A sharp rise in the prices of apartments makes it attractive for developers to invest their money
in building new apartments—because the rate of return to investing in the housing stock is now higher relative to other
ways developers could use their capital. This leads to new construction, which in turn puts downward pressure on rents and
housing prices, as the physical stock of housing increases. Ultimately a long-run equilibrium is reached, in which the rate of
return on investing in one more unit of housing is just equal to
that of investing in similar economic activities with the same
degree of risk. Note finally that the long-run supply of housing is much more elastic than the short-run supply, since there
is ample time in the long run for the physical stock of housing
to respond to price incentives.

Now back to our story of rent control. In 1943, the federal
government imposed rent control as a temporary wartime
measure. Although the federal program ended after the war,
some locations, including New York City, continued the controls on their own. Under New York's controls, a landlord generally could not raise rents on apartments as long as the tenants continued to renew their leases.[1] Rent controls in Santa
Monica are more recent. They were spurred by the inflation of
the 1970s, which, combined with California's rapid population
growth, pushed housing prices and rents to record levels. In
1979, the city of Santa Monica ordered rents rolled back to their
levels of the year before, and stipulated that future rents could
go up by only two-thirds as much as any increase in the overall
price level. In both New York and Santa Monica, the objective
of the controls has been to keep rents below the levels that

---

[1]Since 1974, some apartments in New York have been subject only to more
flexible "rent stabilization" regulations, rather than to absolute rent controls.
The qualitative effects of the two sets of controls are much the same, and so we
do not emphasize the distinction here.

would be observed in freely competitive markets. Achieving this goal has required that both cities impose layer after layer of regulations to prevent landlord and tenant from evading the controls—regulations that are costly to enforce and that distort the normal operation of the market.

In general, the unfettered movement of rental prices in a freely competitive housing market performs three vital functions: Prices allocate existing scarce housing among competing claimants; they promote the efficient maintenance of existing housing, and stimulate the production of new housing, where appropriate; and they ration usage of housing by demanders, thereby preventing wastage of scarce housing. Rent control prevents rental prices from effectively performing these functions. Let's see how.

Rent control discourages the construction of new rental units. Developers and mortgage lenders are reluctant to get involved in building new rental properties because controls artificially depress the most important long-run determinant of profitability—rents. Thus, in one recent year, 11,000 new housing units were built in Dallas, a city with a 16 percent rental vacancy rate but no rent control statute. In that same year, only 2000 units were built in San Francisco, a city with a 1.6 percent vacancy rate but stringent rent control laws. In New York City, except for government-subsidized construction, the only rental units being built are luxury apartments, which are *exempt* from controls.[2] Private construction of new apartments in Santa Monica has also dried up, despite the fact that new office space and commercial developments—both exempt from rent control—are being built at a record pace.

Rent control leads to the deterioration of the *existing* supply of rental housing. When rental prices are held below free

---

[2]While New Yorkers might object to applying the adjective "luxury" to some of the new apartments under construction in the city, the hefty rents that new apartments command suggest that New York tenants must be getting *something* that is not available to the residents of the other 99.99 percent of the American landmass.

market levels, property owners cannot recover through higher rents the costs of maintenance, repairs, and capital improvements. Thus, such activities are sharply curtailed. Eventually, taxes, utilities, and the expenses of the most rudimentary repairs—such as replacing broken windows—overwhelm the depressed rental receipts; as a result, the buildings are abandoned. In New York, some owners have resorted to arson, hoping to collect the insurance on their empty rent-controlled buildings before the city claims them for back taxes. In Santa Monica, the result of rent control is a city of bizarre contrasts: Run-down rental units sit in disrepair next to homes costing $500,000; abandoned apartment buildings share streets with luxury-car dealerships and trendy shops that sell high-fashion clothing to Hollywood stars. Many owners would like to convert their empty buildings to other uses, but to do so, the city insists that they must pay to build new rental units—at a cost of up to $50,000 per apartment—to replace the units they no longer rent. Not surprisingly, few owners have been willing to bear this burden, and so the buildings sit, graffiti-scarred and empty.

Rent control impedes the process of rationing scarce housing. One consequence of this is that tenant mobility is sharply restricted. Even when a family's demand for living space changes—due, say, to a new baby or a teenager's departure for college—there can be substantial costs in giving up a rent-controlled unit. In New York City, where rents can be adjusted when a tenant leaves, moving to a recently vacated apartment can involve a hefty rent hike, even for little or no extra space. In Santa Monica, rents cannot be adjusted when there is a change in tenancy, so landlords often charge "key money" (a large, up-front cash payment) before a new tenant is allowed to move in. The high cost of moving means that large families often stay in cramped quarters while small families, or even single persons, reside in very large units. In New York, this phenomenon of nonmobility has come to be known as "housing gridlock." In Santa Monica, Lena Schunk simply wants to trade places—in her own house—with her downstairs tenant. But she cannot, because Santa Monica regulations require the permission of the tenant, and the tenant doesn't feel like moving upstairs.

Not surprisingly, the distortions produced by rent control lead to efforts by both landlords and tenants to evade the rules. This in turn leads to the growth of cumbersome—and expensive—government bureaucracies whose job it is to make sure the controls *aren't* evaded. In New York, where rents can be raised when tenancy changes hands, landlords have an incentive to make life unpleasant for tenants, or to evict them on the slightest pretense. The city has responded by making evictions extremely costly for landlords. Even if a tenant blatantly and repeatedly violates the terms of a lease, the tenant cannot be evicted if the violations are corrected within a "reasonable" time period. If the violations are not corrected—despite several trips to court by the owners and their attorneys—eviction requires a tedious and expensive judicial proceeding. For their part, tenants routinely try to "sublet" all or part of their rent-controlled apartments at prices substantially above the rent they pay the owner. Since both the city and the landlords try to prohibit subletting, the parties often end up in the city's Housing Courts—an entire judicial system developed chiefly to deal with disputes over rent-controlled apartments.[3]

In Santa Monica, tenants can be evicted, but only after the landlord pays them a "relocation fee" of up to $3000. Even then, the landlord cannot hike the rent for a new tenant. It is little wonder that prospective renters often pay key money of up to $5000 to become tenants—when they are lucky enough to find an apartment available. Even so, the strict controls on monthly rents often force landlords to use other means to discriminate among prospective tenants. Simply to ensure that the rent check comes every month, many landlords rent only

---

[3]Despite the prohibitions on subletting, the practice remains sufficiently widespread that the city has decreed that persons who maintain their tax residence outside New York City forfeit their right to retain rent-controlled apartments—thus opening the way for rent hikes by the landlord.

to well-heeled professionals. As one commentator puts it, "There is no disputing that Santa Monica has become younger, whiter, and richer under rent control."

There is little doubt the bureaucracies that have evolved to administer rent control laws are cumbersome, expensive, and growing. New York City now spends over $150 million a year in its efforts to reclaim buildings abandoned by disgruntled landlords. Even so, derelict buildings are piling up at a record rate. The overflow and appeals from the city's Housing Courts is now clogging the rest of New York's judicial system, impeding the prosecution of violent criminals and drug dealers. In Santa Monica, the annual budget of the Rent Control Board began at $745,000 in 1979 and is now $4.2 million. Its staff has ballooned from 20 people to well over 50 today. And who picks up the tab? The landlords do, of course. In 1989, the annual special assessment levied on them was $144 per unit, up from $84 per unit in 1986.

Ironically, the big losers from rent control—in addition to landlords—are often low-income individuals, especially single mothers. Indeed, many observers now believe that the increasing number of homeless people in cities such as New York and Los Angeles is importantly due to rent controls. Typically, poor individuals can neither afford a hefty key money payment nor assure the discriminating landlord that their rent will be paid on time—much less paid—each month. Since controlled rents generally are well below free-market levels, there is little incentive for apartment owners to take a chance on low-income individuals as tenants. This is especially true if the prospective tenant's chief source of income is a welfare check. Indeed, a significant number of the tenants appearing in New York's Housing Courts are low-income mothers who, due to emergency expenses or delayed welfare checks, have missed rent payments. Often their appeals end in evictions and a new home in temporary public shelters—or on the streets. In Santa Monica, some owners who used to rent one- and two-room units to welfare recipients and other low-income individuals have simply abandoned their buildings, leaving them vacant rather than try to collect artificially depressed rents that fail to cover operating costs. The disgusted owner of one empty and decaying 18-unit building had a friend spray-paint his feelings on the wall: "I want to tear this mess down, but Big Brother won't let me." Perhaps because the owner had escaped from a German concentration camp in search of freedom in America, the friend added a personalized touch: a drawing of a large hammer and sickle.

It is worth noting that the ravages of rent controls are not confined to capitalist nations. In a heavily publicized news conference, the foreign minister of Vietnam, Nguyen Co Thach, recently declared that a "romantic conception of socialism" had destroyed his country's economy after the Vietnam war. Mr. Thach stated that rent control had artificially encouraged demand and discouraged supply, and that all of the housing in Hanoi had fallen into disrepair as a result. Thach concluded by noting, "The Americans couldn't destroy Hanoi, but we have destroyed our city by very low rents. We realized it was stupid and that we must change policy." One can only wonder when the People's Republic of Santa Monica will get the message.

DISCUSSION QUESTIONS

1. Why do you think that governments frequently attempt to control apartment rents but not house prices?
2. What determines the size of the "key money" payments that landlords demand (and tenants offer) for the right to rent a controlled apartment?

16

The Economics of Crime Prevention

How much is crime prevention worth? Plenty, apparently—at least in New York City, which spends over $1.5 *billion* a year on its police department. That works out to about $200 a year for each of the city's residents, or $800 for a family of four. Why do New Yorkers spend so much on crime prevention? If the answer seems obvious, then why don't they spend even *more*? (After all, nearly 2000 murders are committed in New York City each year, and many residents there consider muggings and burglaries as much a part of life as rude taxi drivers.) Would spending more on the police department reduce crime in New York City? If it would, then why did the city council decide to *permit* so much crime—by spending *only* $1.5 billion? If such spending does not deter crime, why wasn't the police department simply abolished, with the savings used, say, to improve the city's decaying school system?

Before we can begin to answer these questions, we must look in greater detail at the economics of fighting crime. First of all, it is not just the police and other law-enforcement agencies that are involved in crime prevention. The courts and the prison system also enter the picture, as do devices such as burglar alarms, locks, and safes. Second, we start with the presumption that spending more on crime prevention makes it more difficult (costly) for people to commit crimes and to avoid detection and punishment. Thus, devoting more resources to law enforcement will, to some degree, deter crime.

Law enforcement has many aspects, and the costs of each must be considered in allocating the resources available. The costs can be divided into three general areas. First there are the costs of the crime detection and the arrest of suspects. Second, costs are involved in the trial and conviction of the prisoner; they vary with the efficiency and speed with which the law-enforcement officials and the courts can act. Third, once sentence is imposed, there are the economic costs of maintaining and staffing prisons. This third area and the social implications of the question of what sorts and durations of punishment are most effective as deterrents to crime are examined in Chapter 23.

Despite the fact that an increase in the amount of resources devoted to discovering and apprehending criminals can be expected to yield a reduction in crime, the optimum allocation of those resources is not so clear-cut. The chief of police or the commissioner is faced with two sets of problems. On the one hand, this individual must decide how to divide the funds between capital and labor—that is, choose either more cars, equipment, and laboratories or more police personnel, detectives, and technicians. On the other hand, the chief must also allocate funds among the various police details within the department—for example, deciding whether to clamp down harder on homicide, on car theft, or on drug traffic.

Within a law-enforcement budget of a given size, the police chief must therefore determine the optimum combination of production factors. The ideal combination is one in which an additional dollar spent on any one of the labor or capital inputs will provide an equal additional amount of crime prevention. If an additional dollar spent on laboratory equipment yields a higher crime-deterrent result than the same dollar spent on a police officer's salary, the laboratory will win. While it is clear that the productivity of inputs is difficult to measure in such small amounts, this does not alter the basic argument. Nor does it alter the argument to say that some inputs are *indivisible*, i.e., come only in fixed, discrete physical units.[1] The police captain must normally judge from experience and intuition as well as from available data whether buying more cars or hiring more men and women will do the better job in checking crime. And this decision may change with changes in relative price. For example, if the salaries of police officers increase, the balance may tip toward the use of more cars or equipment, depending on how well capital can be substituted for labor in a given situation. Instead of using two police officers in a car, it might be economically efficient to equip the car with bulletproof glass and let the driver patrol alone.

The second task of the police chief is to determine how to allocate resources among the interdepartmental details. Sometimes highly publicized events influence this decision. For example, several years ago, prostitution increased in downtown Seattle to such a degree that local merchants complained that streetwalkers were hurting business. The merchants had sufficient political influence to induce the police chief to step up sharply the detection and apprehension of prostitutes. That meant using more personnel and equipment on the vice squad; within the restriction of a fixed budget, this could be done only by pulling resources away from homicide, robbery, and other details, which thus became short-handed.

---

[1]A good or service is said to be indivisible if it can be sold only in relatively large quantities. For example, one cannot purchase one-tenth of a police car. However, perhaps the car can be rented for one-tenth of each month. Given the possibility of rental, many products can no longer be called indivisible.

In effect, the cost of reducing prostitution was a short-run increase in assault and robbery.

We said that three general areas of law enforcement entail costs to society, and we have just dealt with the area of detection and arrest. The second area is the trial and its outcome. Recent studies indicate that the likelihood of conviction is a highly important factor (if not the major one) in the prevention of crime. Currently, the probability of conviction and punishment for crime is extremely low in the United States. Nationwide, the chances of imprisonment for committing a crime are about 1 in 25. In New York City, it has been estimated that an individual who commits a felony faces less than 1 chance in 200 of going to jail. Poor crime detection partly explains such incredible figures; court congestion adds to the problem. In highly urbanized environments, the court calendar is so clogged that the delay in getting a case to trial may stretch from months into years.[2]

One consequence of this situation is an increasing tendency for the prosecutor and suspect to arrange a pretrial settlement rather than further overburden the courts. This is what happens with 90 percent of all criminal charges. Many observers believe that society is underinvesting in the resources needed to improve this process. If more were to be spent on streamlining court proceedings instead of on making arrests, cases could be brought to trial more promptly, the presence of all witnesses could be more easily secured, and the hand of the D.A. would not be forced in making "deals" with suspects. Faced with the probability of quick and efficient trial, a potential criminal might think harder about robbing a bank or mugging a pedestrian. Former Chief Justice Warren E. Burger himself declared that we do in fact need an overhaul of our courts.

---

[2]Many court calendars are solidly booked for two, three, or even five years into the future. In New York, for example, the average time lapse between filing a civil suit and getting it to trial is nearly three and a half *years*.

There remains another issue, which is highly controversial. The likelihood of detection and conviction can be increased by a variety of means, such as wiretapping and changes in the laws protecting the rights of suspects (e.g., permitting law officers to enter and search without knocking, lifting the requirement that suspects be informed of their constitutional rights, and allowing the holding of suspects incommunicado for lengthy periods). We note only that the consequences of such legal changes in terms of infringement on individual liberties are extremely serious, and it is not as yet known how effective such changes would be.

We can now return to our original question. How did New York City determine that a budget of $1.5 billion for crime prevention was the right amount? In the short run, the city was faced with a total budget of a given size and had to decide how to carve it up between law enforcement and other municipal demands, such as fire protection, health, parks, streets, and libraries. Just as a police chief must try to determine what combination of police officers and equipment within a fixed budget will deter the greatest amount of crime, a city council will attempt to choose a combination of spending on all agencies that will yield an amount of public services with the greatest value. If additional money spent on fire protection does not yield as much "good" as it would if spent on police protection, then the amount should be allocated to law enforcement.[3] Determining the value of services rendered by each agency is difficult but not insuperable, at least in principle. Crude approximations can be made of the benefits and costs of crime prevention, and the efficiency of the public sector of our economy can be improved as such calculations are made and refined.

The short-run constraint of a fixed budget for law enforcement may be altered in the long run by asking the state legislature for increased funds for crime prevention. The legis-

---

[3]We assume that the city council equates on the margin returns from money spent on all municipal activities.

lature will then have to wrestle with the same allocation problem that engaged the city council: Will spending an additional dollar on higher education yield greater returns for society than the same dollar given to a city council to allocate to crime prevention? Moreover, the same difficult questions arise in measuring the value of unpriced services resulting from any given state expenditure.

In general, the state will have greater latitude than the city council in raising taxes. If it chooses to hike taxes, this will widen the allocation problem. The increased taxes will reduce the disposable income of some part of the citizenry. Those who pay the additional taxes must in turn decide whether they feel the additional public services made available are worthwhile. For example, is the reduction in crime attributable to an increased expenditure on law enforcement as valuable to them as the goods they could have enjoyed from that increased tax money? If they do not think so, then at the next election they may vote to "throw the rascals out."

Our description indicates that nonmarket solutions to economic problems run basically parallel to market solutions. Although we have focused on crime prevention, the criteria are similar for all types of government decisions and for all levels of government—local, state, and federal. Nevertheless, certain differences must also be noted between decision making in the private, market sector of the economy and in the public, nonmarket sector. Problems of measurement are much greater in the latter. How, for example, do we put a price tag on recreation, which is the output of the parks department? And the signals come through much louder and more clearly in market situations, in which changes in private profitability "telegraph" to entrepreneurs what policies will be best.[4] Instead of market signals, makers of public policy receive a confused set of noises generated by opponents and proponents of their decisions. A legislator is in the unenviable position of

---

[4]In instances where **externalities** exist, it may be to society's advantage to alter these signals by appropriate measures.

trying to please as much of the electorate as possible while operating with very incomplete information.

Some cities have tried to use market mechanisms to improve crime prevention. A few years ago, the city of Orange, California, near Los Angeles, started paying its police according to how much crime was reduced. The incentive scheme applied to four categories of crime—burglary, robbery, rape, and auto theft. Under the plan, as first put into effect, if the crime rate in those categories was cut by a certain amount the previous year, the police would get an extra 1 percent raise. If the crime rate was cut even more, the pay increase would be an extra 2 percent. The results were encouraging. Detectives on their own time produced videotape briefings with leads for patrol officers on specific beats. The whole force developed a campaign to encourage safety precautions in residents' homes. Statistically speaking, the results were even more impressive, for during the first seven months of the program crime in the four target categories fell by almost *triple* the most optimistic goal for the program. The other crime figures held steady, indicating that the police force was not merely shifting its efforts from one area of crime to another.

Consider now a closely related matter. Until the early 1980s, in many cities and states a person beaten up in the streets and left with permanent brain damage could not sue for injuries. The attacker, if caught, would be jailed—but that did not help the victim, who ended up paying taxes for the prisoner's room and board! Victims' rights groups have since made substantial progress, however. The first move toward compensation of victims of crime for their suffering was an initiative passed in California in 1982. This initiative was widely referred to as a "bill of rights" for crime victims. It required convicts to make restitution to those harmed (it also made other broad changes, such as putting limits on bail releases and insanity pleas). Since then, most states have established funds to compensate crime victims. Along the way, Congress passed the Victims of Crime Act, which has distributed millions of dollars collected from federal criminal penalties and fines to victims' groups around the country.

For the most part, however, such compensation is far less than the full cost of the crime. What if a city or a state were obligated for the full cost of a crime committed within its borders? One might guess that unlimited liability on the part of government for crimes against the populace would certainly alter the present allocation of resources between crime prevention and other public endeavors.

This raises the question of what lawyers call "moral hazard." If victims of robberies, for example, were fully compensated by the municipality, there would be less incentive for individuals to protect themselves privately against robberies. The same is true for other crimes. One way to avoid this "moral hazard" is to establish a deductible on the municipality's liability. For example, for home robberies, the municipality might be held responsible for all losses in excess of $500. If this were the case, homeowners still would have an incentive to lock their doors, have watchdogs, and keep lights on at night when away.

Another way in which the allocation of crime-prevention resources might be altered is suggested by a pilot project in crime prevention in Newport News, Virginia, a Navy port city with a population of about 160,000. Aided by a $1.2 million grant from the federal government, the police sought to deter crime before the fact rather than punishing it after the fact. At the heart of the program was a "crime-analysis model," a lengthy questionnaire filled out by police officers whenever a crime was committed. Analysis of these reports over time enabled the police to predict, with a surprising degree of accuracy, where crimes were likely to be committed. Steps could then be taken to prevent the crime, if possible, by drawing on other public and private resources in the community—health clinics, social workers, attorneys, welfare agencies, and so on. By analyzing the 28 cases of homicide over an 18-month period, for example, the police found that 50 percent of all the murders committed had involved family members of the victims and that in half of those cases the police had already had complaints of domestic violence. As a result, a new procedure was implemented. Police began making arrests whenever they witnessed domestic violence, without waiting for a husband or a wife—or other family member—to swear out a warrant. The arrested party was placed in jail and only released if the individual agreed to professional counseling. The counseling seemed to work: For the five years preceding the experiment, the city had averaged 25 murders a year—half of them the result of domestic violence. During the pilot program, however, the murder rate was cut by two-thirds, and domestic murders were reduced even more. In all areas of crime—prostitution, robberies, burglaries, and "nuisance" crimes such as petty theft and vandalism—similar prevention techniques have been used successfully.

Traditionally, police have responded to crime and not taken an active preventive role. The Newport News program involves a radical reorientation of the work of the police officers involved. The results of the experiment suggest that perhaps, if more money and resources were allocated to crime prevention before the fact, the high cost of crime might be reduced—for victims and taxpayers alike.

Crime costs. So does crime prevention. But the latter has benefits to society that should be weighed when making decisions about law-enforcement methods and expenditures.

DISCUSSION QUESTIONS

1. Discuss the allocation of resources for other non-market activities, such as higher education, firefighting, and highway construction.
2. How does a firm decide how to allocate resources? How does it differ from a government agency?

17

More Taxes and Less Work

During much of Ronald Reagan's presidency, government economic policy was dominated by **supply-side economics**, popularly called "Reaganomics." The focus of supply-side economics is on the relationship between taxes and income. Essentially, supply-siders maintain that the *higher* the marginal tax rate, the *lower* the amount of work (and, consequently, income) that is forthcoming. Therefore, if the government would just tax us less, we would work more. Ultimately, the argument goes, the government would benefit in the form of higher tax revenues because incomes would be so much higher. But does this, in fact, really happen?

On its surface, the essence of supply-side economics cannot be faulted. After all, most supply curves slope upward. That is to say, at higher relative prices for a commodity, a larger quantity of the commodity is forthcoming. Therefore, if workers are offered higher *net* wages per marginal unit of work effort, won't they work more? The answer is yes, *most of the time*.

In order to understand the qualification, we have to look at the labor–leisure choices that we all make. Leisure is a good—it generates positive utility for most people. A labor–leisure budget constraint exists for everyone. Think of it in terms of the maximum number of hours (24) that can be "consumed" in any one day. For every hour worked, an hour of leisure (defined as time spent not working) must be given up. The opportunity cost of leisure time, therefore, is a decrease in money income. Put another way, the opportunity cost of leisure is the sacrificed goods and services that extra money income could buy. If a net wage rate is $10 an hour, an extra hour devoted to leisure rather than to work would cost $10—or $10 worth of goods and services.

A *proportional* tax on all labor income reduces the opportunity cost of leisure by an equal amount. For example, if a worker is now earning $10 an hour, a 25 percent income tax on all labor income earned would lower the after-tax wage rate to $7.50 an hour, regardless of the number of hours worked. A *progressive* income tax takes a bigger and bigger bite out of labor income earned, so the opportunity cost of leisure becomes lower as a worker works more and therefore moves into higher tax brackets. Thus, both a proportional and a progressive tax on labor income lower after-tax income and therefore lower the opportunity cost of leisure, but by differing amounts at different numbers of hours worked.

It seems straightforward that an increase in tax rates, which decreases the opportunity cost of leisure, would decrease the number of hours worked. And if this is so, the converse should also be true—that is, a *reduction* in tax rates should *increase* the number of hours worked and, consequently, the total income in the economy. This would be the logical result of what we have been examining: the **substitution effect** of a change in the price of working. As tax rates fall, workers substitute work for leisure.

But there is another effect occurring at the same time. It can be best illustrated by what happened to American companies that embarked on large-scale development projects in Algeria when that country became independent from France in 1962. Wage rates in Algeria at the time were perhaps one-tenth of what they were in the United States for comparable work. Although American companies weren't about to pay Algerian laborers American wages, they saw no reason to pay what seemed to be the abysmally low wages commonly received by manual laborers in that country. Instead, they offered a wage rate that was perhaps one-third of what it would be in the United States but effectively three to four times more than what the ordinary Algerian wage earner typically made. Now, supply-side economics would lead us to predict that at those relatively high wage rates, Algerian laborers would want to work more, not less. But this didn't happen. Much to the chagrin of the American managers, large parts of their labor force would simply not show up for work after having worked a short period of time. Why not? Because those workers had obtained the equivalent of one or two years' worth of income in a very short period. Therefore, they could afford to "buy" large amounts of leisure—which they chose to do.

What the American companies experienced was what economists call the **income effect** of a change in wages. At some point, the individual's supply curve of labor is "backward bending." That is, when effective after-tax wage rates are increased to higher and higher levels, an income effect takes over: The increased income makes a person feel richer, and thus that individual is motivated to buy more leisure, not less—even though the opportunity cost of buying more leisure has increased. When this income effect overrides the substitution effect, the individual's labor supply curve becomes backward bending, i.e., less labor is supplied at higher wages. Thus, we would predict that if marginal tax rates are decreased more and more, this will eventually cause workers to work less, not more—contrary to supply-side theory.

The Reagan administration relied on supply-side theory in concluding that tax rates should be cut, particularly for higher-income groups, to produce more economic activity and thereby more tax revenue. The enactment in 1981 of the Kemp-Roth tax plan, which reduced income taxes by 25 percent in three stages, was the legislative highlight of supply-side economics. But the very large deficits that resulted when the economy did not rebound quickly enough from the recession of the early 1980s called into question the practical effects of supply-side theory, and the Reagan administration retreated from sole reliance on tax reductions to stimulate economic growth. Nonetheless, the administration still hoped that other tax-reform measures in the 1980s, particularly the Tax Reform Act of 1986, would yield not only a fairer taxation system, but also, in the long run, increased revenue for government as a result of slightly lower overall tax rates for some taxpayers. Unfortunately, as yet we don't have much evidence on how effective supply-side economics might be if, in fact, marginal tax rates were significantly lowered for most of the American population. And although President Bush promised "no new taxes," the perennial budget crises that have afflicted Washington mean that the lower marginal tax rates that might produce such evidence are unlikely in the forseeable future.

DISCUSSION QUESTIONS

1. What other substitution effects can result from high marginal tax rates? (Hint: What about do-it-yourself projects around the home?)
2. Do you think the Tax Reform Act of 1986 will create increased tax revenues in the long run because of the lower overall tax rates for some American taxpayers?

Part Four

Social Issues
and Externalities

INTRODUCTION

Many issues in our society do not lend themselves to strict supply-demand analysis. Typically these issues involve what are called *externalities*; that is, either the costs or the benefits—or both—of some economic activity are external to the decision-making process of those who are generating them. An example of a negative externality is air pollution. Externalities, whether negative or positive, typically occur because of a common-property problem. **Common property** is property that at one and the same time is owned by no one and by everyone. Air and, to a lesser extent, water have been treated as common property for many years. Since no one effectively owns common property, no one has an incentive to efficiently use (or not abuse) it.

Chapter 18 emphasizes the importance of assessing the full spectrum of costs involved when implementing broad social policies such as the war on drugs. The lack of property rights is the central issue in the chapters on animal extinction, oil spills, and clamming (Chapters 19, 20, and 21, respectively). These are all social issues involving **social costs** and benefits. An explicit attempt to create property rights in the ability to pollute is discussed in Chapter 22, while Chapter 23 offers a cost/benefit analysis of crime and punishment.

All of the issues discussed in this part demonstrate the power of economic analysis. Social issues have a way of becoming economic issues, because they typically involve decisions about how to use scarce resources.

18

The Social Costs of Drug Wars

One can think of many reasons why a society might wish to prohibit, regulate, or restrain an activity. Most of these reasons fall into one of two classes. The first class focuses on *informational factors*. Society judges that certain (perhaps all) of its members do not have the information, judgment, or wisdom to make informed decisions about certain activities. The second class of reasons for proscribing or limiting behavior focuses on the *external effects* of that behavior: Some activities have consequences that impinge not just on the person engaging in that activity, but on other members of society as well.

Consider, for example, society's decision to prohibit the use of drugs such as marijuana, cocaine, and heroin. To varying degrees, these drugs are viewed by many members of society as having addictive properties; that is, after some period of using the drug, users become *unable* to stop consuming them,

135

despite costs of continued use that clearly far exceed the benefits.[1] In general, it is argued, the amount of "safe" (nonaddic-
tive) use varies among individuals, and is unknown for each
person before the fact. Moreover, once the line of addiction
has been crossed, the affected individuals are no longer able to
act in their own self-interest, as normally defined.[2] Thus, to
protect individuals from themselves, i.e., to prevent them
from inadvertently becoming addicted, society prohibits *any*
use of the drugs.

Prohibition of drugs such as marijuana, cocaine, and heroin is also justified on the basis of preventing people from in-
flicting harm on *other members of society*—harm that the perpetrators would not inflict if they bore the full costs of their
actions. Heroin addicts, for example, commonly finance their
habits by committing "property" crimes, such as larcenies,
burglaries, car thefts, mugging, and the like, obviously imposing costs not only on the victims (and potential victims), but
also on the taxpayers who must finance additional police and
prison expenditures. Women who are heavy users of cocaine
during pregnancy frequently give birth to infants who are
both addicted to cocaine and suffering from a variety of birth
defects. Simply ensuring the short-term survival of such
babies is estimated to cost an average of $90,000 each, a cost
generally borne by taxpayers. Moreover, it is believed that
many of these babies ultimately will turn out to have sufficient
physical or mental impairments that they will be heavily de-

---

[1]We do not wish to debate whether, for example, marijuana is "really" ad
dictive, or the extent to which particular addictions are psychological or physiological. For the reader who doubts the existence or nature of addictions to a
particular drug, we suggest thinking in terms of heroin—about which both
the existence of and physiological nature of the addiction seem universally
agreed upon.

[2]Recovering addicts and alcoholics commonly report: (1) having no prior
intention of becoming addicted; (2) being unable (for an extended period of
time) to stop usage, once addicted; (3) having done things while addicted that
were "irrational," in the sense that in retrospect, the costs greatly exceeded the
benefits; and (4) a great sense of relief that they are recovering from their
affliction.

pendent on the rest of society, throughout their lives. In each of these examples, drug users do not bear the full costs of their actions, and so engage in "too much" drug use, in the sense that the social costs exceed the benefits. Thus, just as society prohibits businesses from engaging in certain forms of air and water pollution because of the costs they impose on other individuals, society prohibits the use of certain drugs.[3]

If arguments such as these are valid—and for our present purposes, we accept them as such—there remains another matter. Presumably, restrictions on what we consume, on how we behave in public, and the like are imposed because they yield some benefits. When informational factors are the rationale, these benefits are conferred on the person whose behavior is constrained—the potential addict, for example, is spared the agony of addiction. When there are external costs involved, the restrictions benefit persons other than those whose behavior is restricted—our taxes are lower, for example, and we need not be afraid to go out at night. But whoever may be the beneficiaries of these restrictions, *the benefits can be achieved only at some cost.*

Recognizing that it is costly to prohibit certain activities does *not* (necessarily) mean that we should refrain from prohibiting them. It does, however, mean that we must ask whether the benefits of the prohibition outweigh the costs. It also means that, even if the prohibition of an activity is the *ideal*, we must decide how close to the ideal we should strive to get. With these thoughts in mind, let's take a look at the costs of prohibiting the consumption of drugs such as marijuana, cocaine, and heroin.

Consider first the direct costs of enforcing the laws against these drugs. New York City currently spends in excess of $600 million a year—about $80 for each resident of the

---

[3]In some cases, both informational factors and the imposition of external costs may be involved—as clearly seems to be the case with heroin. Neither the fact that there may be multiple motives for the same restriction nor the possibility that it may be difficult to disentangle them diminishes the usefulness of the conceptual distinction between the two motives.

city—enforcing drug laws. Of the 18,000 people currently in New York City jails, about half are there on drug-related charges. The federal government spends about $8 billion a year enforcing drug laws, and it is estimated that nearly 40 percent of the 55,000 prisoners in federal prisons are there on drug-related charges. Nationwide, government spending on drug-law enforcement at all levels is believed to be in the neighborhood of $20 billion a year—and growing rapidly.

Despite these expenditures and imprisonments, the legal authorities have had remarkably little success in making major inroads on drug consumption. Not even the most optimistic government officials claim they are stopping more than 15 percent of the illegal drugs from getting through, and most observers peg the interdiction rate at less than 10 percent. An important reason for the relatively low productivity of enforcement dollars is the nature of the crime itself. Illegal drug deals bring together willing buyers and willing sellers, both of whom view themselves as *benfiting* from the illegal act that is taking place. In popular parlance, drug deals are "victimless" crimes—at least as perceived by the parties involved. As a result, the legal authorities must proceed without what is generally believed to be the most important ingredient in a successful prosecution—the victim.

The retail value of the illegal drugs sold in the United States is widely estimated to be *at least* $150 billion a year, and many observers put the figure at $200 billion or more.[4] Odd as it may seem, the magnitude of the amount of money involved in the illegal drug trade is, importantly, *caused* by the fact that the drugs are illegal. Government attempts to prevent the sale of drugs drive up the costs of selling them and thus reduce the supply of the drugs. In turn, this pushes the price of drugs up and reduces the consumption of drugs—which, of course, is the point. But this is not the full story.

---

[4]As of 1988, the estimated annual street value of marijuana *alone* was $20 billion. See Mark A. R. Kleiman, *Marijuana: Costs of Abuse, Costs of Control* (New York: Greenwood Press, 1989).

The demand for drugs such as marijuana, cocaine, and heroin is *inelastic*, which means that an *x* percent increase in the price of the drugs will result in a reduction in consumption that is *less* than *x* percent. The consequence must be a *rise* in expenditures on the drugs. Consider, for example, marijuana. It has been estimated that the *elasticity of demand* for marijuana is about −0.4, which means that a 10 percent increase in its price (caused, say, by more enforcement) will cause a reduction in consumption of about 4 percent but will also cause a *rise* in expenditures on marijuana of about 6 percent. Thus, every time enforcement efforts are stepped up, illegal drug expenditures by consumers—and revenues of suppliers—increase.[5]

This facet of illegal drugs has a costly consequence, illustrated by the example of heroin, one of the most addictive drugs in existence. Partly as a result of the drug's addictive properties, the demand for heroin is extremely inelastic. Even a small reduction in the supply of heroin causes a large increase in expenditures on the drug by addicts, many of whom as we said earlier, finance their habits by committing "property" crimes such as burglaries, robberies, car thefts, shoplifting, and mugging. The result is that efforts to cut heroin supplies have trivial effect on the consumption of heroin (due to the inelastic demand) but yield a large increase in expenditures on heroin—and thus a large increase in the property crimes used to finance those expenditures. In an important sense, "crime prevention" becomes crime creation.

The illegal status of drugs such as marijuana, cocaine, and heroin produces a peculiar cost structure in the industry. The "tax" of criminal prosecution that is levied on suppliers ends up being applied unevenly; some dealers are caught, while others are not. Those who are detected and prosecuted

---

[5]Since expenditures equal price times quantity, the percentage change in expenditures will equal the sum of the percentage change in price and the percentage change in quantity. Because we are dealing here with a movement *along* the demand curve, caused by a *shift* of the supply curve, the price and quantity changes must be oppositely signed.

are big losers. On average, gross profit margins must (in equilibrium) compensate dealers for this risk. But this means that those who happen to be lucky enough or skillful enough to avoid prosecution end up earning enormous profits. Pharmaceutical-grade cocaine costs about $20 an ounce to manufacture; cut to a purity level of, say, 40 percent and sold on the streets of Los Angeles, that cocaine has a retail value of $5000. Marijuana growers in Kentucky (which ranks third in pot production, behind California and Oregon) estimate that they clear between $600 and $1000 *per plant*, depending on its size. Heroin that wholesales for $170,000 can easily bring $500,000 at the retail level in New York City.

Profits like these engender pushers—and the potential for both corruption and violence. Consider an importer who is bringing in 500–1000 kilograms (kilos) of cocaine at a time, and selling to primary wholesalers in lots of 10–50 kilos. Each *successful* sale can bring gross profits of $250,000. But there are several obstacles between the seller and the profits: First, the transaction is illegal, so the police may prove troublesome. To ensure the success of the sale, the seller may wish to pay the police to "look the other way." Such incentives were present during Prohibition, and payoffs by bootleggers to police are well documented. Over the last decade, drug-related police corruption has become equally well documented. Recently, in one year alone, twelve New York City police officers were arrested on drug-related corruption charges, and seven Miami police officers were indicted on similar charges. Some observers have argued that drug-related police corruption is currently present to varying degrees in virtually *every* major city in the country and in many small jurisdictions as well.

The illegal nature of drugs also fosters violence. Whenever exchange occurs there is the possibility that one of the parties may find it advantageous to renege on the deal: The seller may deliver a product that fails to match the quantity or quality promised, or the buyer may fail to pay. Sometimes the risk of such "cheating" can be avoided by establishing a regular, long-term buyer–seller relationship. In such cases, the value of the *continuing* relationship exceeds what either party could gain from cheating on any *one* transaction, and so the individual transactions become effectively "self-enforcing." Another way to avoid the risk of being cheated on the transaction is to deal with parties who have established reputations in their dealings with others. "Reputable" buyers and sellers will avoid cheating even new customers, because to do so would damage their credibility with other traders, once word got out. Finally, even if measures such as these fail and a contract violation results, the damaged party may be able to appeal to the legal authorities for redress.

For the buyers and sellers of illegal drugs, all of these means of preventing cheating are made more difficult. Attempts to establish long-term trading relationships are often disrupted by the police, who haul one or both of the parties off to jail. Reputations are more difficult to establish, partly because advertising is likely to bring more cops than customers. Moreover, buyers and sellers actually have incentives to *hide* their identities from each other, so that if one is subsequently arrested, he or she cannot "shop" (reveal the identity of) the other to police. Finally, of course, in the event one party to a drug deal cheats, the other party effectively cannot appeal to the legal authorities for assistance. Illegal contracts are not enforceable at law; besides, few drug dealers would be so stupid as to tell the police their buyer walked off without paying.

Similar considerations imply that legal means of *competition* are more costly in the drug trade. Advertising and the establishment of convenient, regular times and places of business are more costly, because they increase the chances of detection and prosecution. Even price cutting as a means of competition becomes less effective, because information about the existence of lower prices is so costly to disseminate.

The high cost of *legal* means of competition and contract enforcement induces buyers and sellers of drugs to turn to *illegal* means—the most effective of which is violence. This in turn attracts people to the industry who have a comparative advantage in committing violence. As we noted in Chapter 1, just as the bootlegger's Thompson submachine was often the low-cost means of conducting business during Prohibition, so too is the drug dealer's MAC-10 machine gun today. Over the last several years, cities across the country—from Miami to Los Angeles to Washington, D.C.—have reported sharp increases in the number of "drug-related" murders, assaults with firearms, and other acts of violence. Sometimes the targets are other parties in drug deals "gone bad," or competitors engaged in "turf battles"; other times, the victims are simply innocent bystanders, caught in the wrong place at the wrong time. Most of the time, however, the cause is the same: The illegal nature of the product has eliminated legal means of settling disputes, so the parties turn to the next-best alternative—violence.

Choices involve both benefits and costs. Good choices require that both benefits and costs be correctly and completely taken into account. Most would agree that the benefits of prohibiting the use of drugs such as marijuana, cocaine, and heroin are substantial, both to would-be users and to other members of society. Yet it is becoming increasingly clear that these benefits come at the expense of substantial costs.

The famous Civil War general William Tecumseh Sherman maintained that "war is hell," a pronouncement that seems just as valid when the nature of the enemy is pharmacological rather than human. Sixty years ago, Americans weighed the benefits and costs of prohibiting the use of alcohol, and decided that the costs were simply too high. Whether Americans will—or should—make that same decision regarding illicit drugs we cannot say. But we can say that when decisions regarding the war on drugs are made, both the benefits and the costs must be correctly and completely weighed if the choices are to be good ones.

DISCUSSION QUESTIONS

1. It is estimated that alcohol kills a minimum of 200,000 Americans each year. Cocaine is implicated in the

deaths of only a few thousand people a year. Why do we permit the consumption of alcohol but not the consumption of cocaine? Even more striking comparisons can be made regarding tobacco and marijuana. Ask yourself the same question for these two goods.

2. Are the decisions we have made regarding alcohol and tobacco relevant to our decisions about other drugs? (Hint: Crossing the street is dangerous. Does the fact that we cross on a green light mean we should also cross when the light is red?)

19

A Farewell to Elephants: The Economics of Extinction

In its report on the Endangered Species Act, the Senate Commerce Committee concluded that the two principal causes of animal extinction are hunting and destruction of habitat. There is certainly an element of truth in this observation: Ever since prehistoric times humans and animals have competed for space and habitat on this planet. The problem, however, is more complex than a simple statement of that sort.

Let us begin with prehistoric times. The destruction of animal species by humans is nothing new. The arrival of human beings in North America about 12,000 years ago is usually tied to the extinction of most of the existing mega-fauna. The LaBrea Tarpits yielded 24 mammals and 22 birds that no longer exist. Among these are the saber-tooth tiger, the giant llama, the 20-foot ground sloth, and a bison that stood 7 feet at the hump with 6-foot-wide horns.

In fact, only 0.02 percent of all the species that have ever existed on earth are currently extant. While many believe that human hunting was directly responsible for the destruction of these species, there is some evidence to the contrary.

The argument for direct human guilt in destroying animal species is based on the veiw that humans were indiscriminate, wasteful hunters. Hunting methods such as driving animals over a cliff, which resulted in many more being killed than could be used by the tribe, are said to be illustrations of this indiscriminate destruction of male and female and healthy and crippled animals alike. The fact that no group had exclusive property rights over animals while those animals were *alive* meant there was little incentive to keep the animals alive for later harvesting. If one group was careful and husbanded the animals, another group would simply exploit them in competition with that group.

This view has not gone unchallenged. Some have argued that, in fact, primitive tribes did husband the resource by attempting to kill off only the weaker animals, and taking care to preserve the females of the species. But note that the issue was still one of the lack of property rights to live animals. Most of the species in question occupied habitats up to several hundred square miles in size, and many were migratory. In any event, "ownership" of specific animals typically could be established only by killing them. Live animals were fair game, so to speak. To the degree that the animals were exclusively within the hunting range of only one tribe, that tribe had an incentive to husband the resource and to provide for a perpetual renewal of those animals. But when the animals ranged over the lands of several tribes, no tribe had any incentive to protect the future interests of other, competing tribes, and could not—short of open warfare—protect their own future interests against the ravages of their neighbors.

Whether or not primitive tribes in America were responsible for the extinction of many early animals and birds is still an open question, but the role of human beings in the extinction of animals at a later time is much clearer. The first known instance is the extinction of the European lion, the last survivor being dated to A.D. 80. In modern times the most famous example is the passenger pigeon. At one time these birds were the most numerous species of birds in North America and perhaps in the world. They nested and migrated together in huge flocks, and probably numbered in the billions. When flocks passed overhead, the sky would be dark with pigeons, for days at a time. Audubon measured one roost at 40 miles long and about 3 miles wide. While the Indians had long hunted these birds, it was the arrival of the white man and the demand for pigeons as a source of food and sport that led to their ultimate demise. The birds were netted and shot in vast numbers. And by the end of the nineteenth century, an animal species that had been looked on as indestructible because of its enormous numbers had almost completely disappeared. The last known passenger pigeon died in the Cincinnati Zoo in 1914.

The American bison only narrowly escaped the same fate. The vast herds that roamed the plains were an easy target for hunters; with the advent of the railroad and the need to feed railroad crews as transcontinental railroad lines were built, hunters such as Buffalo Bill Cody killed bison by the thousands. Then, as the demand for the fur of the bison increased, it became the target for still further hunting. Like the passenger pigeon, the bison appeared to be indestructible because of its numbers. But in the absence of any property rights over live bison, the result was almost the same as with the passenger pigeon—bison were becoming extinct. Despite the outcries of the Indians who found their major food source being decimated, it was not until late in the nineteenth century that any efforts were made to protect the bison.[1]

---

[1]For the bison's cousin, the eastern buffalo—which stood seven feet tall at the shoulder, was twelve feet long, and weighed more than a ton—the efforts came too late. The last known members of the species—a cow and her calf—were killed in 1825 in the Allegheny Mountains.

The fate of the passenger pigeon and the near demise of the bison illustrate the main dilemma of protecting endangered species. To the degree that there are no ownership rights over these animals, anyone can attempt to hunt them for private gain. The conflict between the needs of human beings for food and clothing and the survival of a particular species can only lead to one end—the extinction of the animal species.

In modern times, government has attempted, by means of state and federal regulation, to limit hunting seasons and the number of animals or birds that may be taken. The results have been at least partially successful. It is probable that there are more deer in North America today than there were at the time of the colonists. The same is true for a number of other animal species. In effect, a rationing system (rather than prices) was used to limit the exploitation of a "common-property resource." But the threatened extinction in modern times of many species of whales illustrates that the problem is far from resolved.

The pattern of harvesting whales has been the subject of international discussion ever since World War II. It was readily apparent to all concerned that without some form of restraint the whaling population was in danger of extinction. The result was the founding of an international regulatory body, the International Whaling Commission (IWC), in 1948, in an attempt to regulate international whaling through cooperative endeavor. But the IWC was virtually doomed from the start. Its members were given the right to veto any regulation they considered too restrictive; if a member decided to blatantly disobey the regulations, the IWC had no enforcement powers. Since some whaling nations, such as Chile and Peru, refused to join the IWC, quotas had little effect on these nations. And some IWC members have used nonmember flagships to circumvent the quotas themselves, or have simply claimed that they were killing the animals for exempt "research" purposes.

The story of the decimation of a species is probably best told in the events surrounding the blue whale. Even with the most modern equipment, the great blue whale, which some-times weighs almost a hundred tons, is difficult to kill; nev-ertheless, intensive hunting methods gradually reduced the stock from somewhere between 300,000 and 1 million to, at present, somewhere between 600 and 3000. In the 1930–1931 winter season, almost 30,000 blue whales were taken. As a result of intensive harvesting, fewer than 10,000 were taken by 1945–1946, and in the late 1950s the yearly catch was down to around 1500 a year. By 1964–1965, the total was only 20 whales. In 1965, the IWC placed a ban on killing blue whales. But even after the ban, the hunting of blues continued from land stations by nonmembers such as Brazil, Chile, and Peru.

Humpback whales have suffered a similar fate. From an original population estimated at 300,000, there remain be-tween 1500 and 5000 today. Like the blues, humpbacks are now under a hunting ban, but the lack of monitoring capacity makes it probable that the ban is only nominal. The problems of the IWC can be seen in the reactions to several conservation measures passed at one IWC annual meeting. The United States pushed through measures banning the hunting of fin-backs in the Antarctic, setting the quota on minke whales at 5000 instead of 12,000 as Japan requested, and instituting an area-by-area quota for sperm whales so that the total popula-tion would be protected. A year later, the Japanese and then the Russians, parties to these agreements, announced they would set more realistic quotas in line with Japanese interests.

Moreover, even where government regulations attempt to protect animals, poaching, a lucrative source of income, has been widespread. This is particularly true in poor nations: To an individual native hunter in Africa, the income from the ivory tusks of a single elephant may be the difference between starvation and relative abundance. Between 1981 and 1989 the population of African elephants was cut to 600,000 from 1.2 million, and a pair of average-size tusks weighing 20 pounds now brings about $6000 on the wholesale market. In African nations where average *annual* income is but a few hundred dollars per person, it is little wonder that the African elephant is a prime target of poachers.

The precarious future of the African elephant also reveals that the actions of host governments often play a pivotal role in determining the survival chances of an endangered species. In South Africa and Zimbabwe, where strong governments allow controlled culls (at hefty fees) and plow the proceeds into protecting the herds from poachers, elephant populations are growing. The nation of Burundi, which exports more than 20,000 elephant tusks each year, provides a sharp contrast. Internationally recognized elephant counts reveal that only one (yes, one) elephant actually lives in Burundi. Nevertheless, year after year, the government of that nation certifies that all of the country's tusk exports are harvested within Burundi's borders rather than poached elsewhere. One can only wonder how that solitary, prolific pachyderm does it—and what share of the profits might be going to government officials. Many experts feel that, without a significant reduction in poaching throughout the continent, the African elephant faces extinction within the next 10 to 20 years.

Nothing better illustrates the dilemma of animal extinction than the cases of the snail darter and of the coyote. The National Environmental Policy Act of 1969 made it mandatory that an environmental impact statement be prepared on all projects that would affect the environment. A mechanism was thus created for the protection of endangered species against environmental destruction. The snail darter is a small fish whose existence was threatened by the construction of a dam proposed by the Tennessee Valley Authority (TVA). The environmental impact statement process required the TVA to list the extinction of the snail darter as the probable outcome of the construction of the dam. The 1973 Endangered Species Act, with its clause requiring emergency action to protect any species threatened with extinction, was invoked. The result was a national furor in which the benefits to humankind of the additional power to be provided by the dam were measured against the possible extinction of an obscure small fish whose existence was known only to a very small number of people. This issue was resolved when the TVA reevaluated the benefit costs of the dam and concluded that the dam was not worthwhile after all. Nevertheless, many people viewed the conflict as an absurd one in terms of the benefit costs of a snail darter versus hydroelectric power—particularly when it was later learned that the snail darter was thriving in many other locations and whose species survival was thus not even threatened by the dam.

However, if the snail darter illustrates an absurdity in the efforts to save animals from extinction, the case of coyote versus sheep highlights a more difficult dilemma. The coyote has not come under protection, but the ways by which it can be hunted have been severely limited; in particular, some methods of poisoning the coyote have been restricted or forbidden, with the result that there has been an enormous growth in their population. Lamb is a favorite food of the coyote. Consequently, the sheepherders in many areas have found it prohibitively expensive to raise sheep because of their decimation by a growing coyote population. With fewer sheep, the relative prices of wool and lamb have risen significantly in the United States. What should be the outcome? Should the coyote be protected, as many environmental groups have insisted, and are we willing to pay the price of substantially higher costs for wool and lamb as a result? The conflict between human and animal species is not easily resolved, as these two cases illustrate.

DISCUSSION QUESTIONS

1. Has there ever been a problem of the extinction of dogs, cats, or cattle? Why not?
2. Some argue that the only way to save rare species is to set up private game reserves to which wealthy hunters can travel. How could this help save endangered species?

20

Oil Pollution, Obvious and Otherwise

Stars filled the night sky on March 23, 1989, as the oil tanker *Exxon Valdez* steamed south, bound for California with more than 100 million gallons of Alaskan crude oil aboard. At 11:50 P.M. the captain of the *Valdez* turned over control of the vessel to the third mate; as the skipper left the bridge, he ordered the mate to make a right turn at 11:55 P.M. so as to keep the ship well clear of a rocky outcrop known as Bligh Reef. The captain's order in fact was not executed until 12:02 A.M.—too late to prevent what followed. At 12:08 A.M. the *Exxon Valdez* struck Bligh Reef; the rocks quickly sliced open the ship's forward compartments, spilling some 240,000 barrels of viscous crude oil—more than 10 million gallons—into the pristine waters of Alaska's Prince William Sound. Within a week the oil slick covered more than 900 square miles, killing and maiming marine mammals, fish, and migratory wildfowl. By mid-April the slick, grown in size to 1600 square miles, was threatening wild-life in the Kenai Peninsula National Park, hundreds of miles southwest of Bligh Reef. Before summer's end, the Exxon Corp. estimated it had already spent more than $1 billion on cleanup efforts—and despaired of recovering even 10 percent of the crude that had escaped the hold of the *Valdez*.

While the disaster that struck the *Exxon Valdez* was the first major spill of North Slope oil since the Alaskan pipeline opened in 1977, it was neither the first nor even the biggest supertanker spill to damage the world's oceans. Eleven years before, almost to the day, the supertanker *Amoco Cadiz* had run aground off the coast of France, disgorging 68 million gallons of crude oil into the icy sea. More than 130 miles of French coastline were polluted, causing damages estimated at more than $2 billion. Even the *Cadiz* incident was but the capstone of a string of serious spills during the oil-crazed 1970s, as nations around the world proved willing to go to almost any lengths to get their hands on petroleum.

In the years that passed between the *Cadiz* and *Valdez* spills, the specter of giant tankers wreaking ecological havoc largely faded—even though at the beginning of the 1980s, the term *oil pollution* had become almost synonymous with *supertanker*. In the mid-1970s, when escalating oil prices created a demand for cheaper ways of transporting crude oil, super-tankers had emerged as the apparent solution. Some of these sea mammoths cost as much as $100 million to build and were so large that crew members used motorbikes to get from one end of the ship to the other. The largest was nearly one-third of a mile long and weighed nearly 565,000 tons.[1] Accidental oil spills from these enormous tankers—such as the one in 1978 and several earlier ones—caused scientists and others to become gravely concerned about the welfare of our planet's oceans and marine life.

---

[1]When fully loaded, the *Exxon Valdez* is "only" 987 feet long and 166 feet wide. By way of comparison, that's longer than three football fields and wider than a 12-lane expressway.

During the 1980s, however, the threat of oil spills from supertankers was reduced by forces in the marketplace. As a result of sharp declines in oil prices during the first half of the decade, many supertankers became obsolete. Increasingly, they were replaced by more profitable, smaller tankers, leaving the high seas to be disassembled in wrecking yards or used for storage.[2] In a report issued not long before the *Exxon Valdez* disaster, the National Research Council concluded that oil spills were contributing less to the petroleum content in our oceans than were routine tanker operations and municipal and other wastes. Although the Council's conclusion may have to be reassessed in light of the *Valdez* spill, the fact remains that *major* spills became a far less important contributor to oil pollution during the 1980s.

Indeed, despite the headlines devoted to major spills, a greater potential concern today is far more ordinary: The pollution of our groundwater supplies by gasoline and other petroleum products caused by leakage from underground storage tanks. Studies show that the "safe" life of an underground steel tank is approximately 15 years and that at least half of all the tanks that have been underground for a longer period are now leaking. One oil industry expert has estimated that nearly one-third of the nation's 1 million-plus service-station tanks may be leaking today.

This **negative externality** of the retail oil industry is a costly one for water users. Health hazards caused by drinking gasoline-polluted water include anemia, kidney disease, disorders of the nervous system, and cancer. Even bathing in such polluted water can be harmful. For example, benzene—one of the nearly 300 chemicals contained in gasoline—can be absorbed through the skin during a bath. The result of such a bath would be much the same as drinking benzene-polluted water. Showering in such water also can create chemical vapors that might result in skin and eye irritation.

[2]Saudi Arabia, for example, uses a small fleet of anchored supertankers to store grain rather than bothering to build silos.

The problem of this form of water pollution is complicated by the fact that underground water is essentially a *common-property resource*. To a certain extent, it is like air: Nobody owns it and everybody can use it. This means that even if a service-station owner, for example, knew that an underground gas tank was old and very likely leaking, that proprietor would have no incentive to incur the high cost of replacing the tank unless he or she were being affected by the polluted water. One might hope that the gas-station owner would let humane motives govern his or her actions and replace the tank to prevent further water pollution, even though it would prove very costly. Economic theory predicts, however, that unless the benefits to an individual from a potential action outweigh the costs, that action very likely will not be undertaken. And unless the health of the service-station owner in this case is immediately threatened by the water being polluted, the benefits may not be perceived to be greater than the costs.

What can be done to keep further oil pollution from occurring? One obvious solution is to make the polluters pay in the form of liability lawsuits for damages. But determining who the polluting culprit is can sometimes be a difficult matter, especially in a large metropolitan area where several underground tanks are located in the same vicinity. Assessing the costs in such a case is also complicated. How do you place a price tag on illnesses caused by water pollution? And how can it be demonstrated, beyond a reasonable doubt, that certain illnesses are the result of polluted water and not some other factor? In principle, these determinations can be made. But in practice, the task is far from simple.

Indeed, considerations such as these suggest that there may be certain "advantages" to oil pollution from spills such as that caused by the *Exxon Valdez*. The source of the pollutant is immediately apparent, and the parties responsible are generally readily identifiable. (So unmistakable were the facts in the case of the *Exxon Valdez*, for example, that within a matter of weeks the Exxon Corp. had already set aside more than $1 billion to cover initial clean-up costs.) Moreover, a larger component of the damages in the case of major spills is due to acute (massive, short-term) exposure rather than to chronic (low-intensity, long-term) exposure; thus the nature and magnitude of the damages, as well as liability, are easier to assess. Such facts, of course, do not lessen the great harm done by such spills, but they do make it easier to punish those responsible and thus make future violations less likely.

One obvious solution to the problem of hidden, chronic damage done by leaking tanks is to enact state or federal legislation mandating the replacement of all underground tanks every 15 years. Such legislation, however, would not be without costs to society. One of the consequences of such laws would be the increased taxes necessary to pay for policing and enforcement of replacement requirements. Another cost would be a higher price for gasoline. This is because the purchase and installation of new gas tanks is a very costly undertaking, and some of those additional costs incurred by oil companies and service-station owners would be passed on to consumers. Rich and poor alike use gasoline, but it represents a larger proportion of the expenditures of the poor.[3] Hence, a greater burden would fall on low-income groups. Legislation of this type would also very likely mean the disappearance of many of the smaller service stations owned and operated by independent dealers, who can ill afford the additional cost required by tank replacements. The million or so independent dealers currently in business across the nation offer competition to the major oil companies and a convenience to Americans that might be reduced if such laws are passed.

In short, a solution to the problem of oil pollution of our underground water supply is not simple, nor is it likely to be without cost. Whether we like it or not, safe drinking water is

[3]Studies have shown the following distribution of gasoline expenditures as a proportion of annual income: $6000–$10,000 income, 3.4 percent; $10,000–$14,000 income, 3.3 percent; $14,000–$30,000 income, less than 2 percent; above $30,000, 1.4 percent.

becoming a scarce good, and like other scarce commodities, it may well have a higher price tag in the future.

DISCUSSION QUESTIONS

1. Can you think of solutions, other than government legislation, to the problem of underground water pollution?
2. Does the problem of water pollution differ in any way from the problem of air pollution?

21

Clamming and Other "Free" Goods

The razor clam (*Siliqua patula*) is a large bivalve of the Solenidae family that inhabits the ocean beaches of the Pacific Coast from California to Alaska. Once a major staple of the coastal Indian population, it is now a major prey of people escaping the city for the ocean beaches. (Cleaned, cut into steaks, dipped in batter, fried one minute on each side, and served with a bottle of dry white wine, it is superb.)

These clams are dug in minus tides, and the beach area they inhabit is not, at least in the state of Washington, private property. Therefore, access is available to everyone, and the only costs of digging clams are time, cut fingers, and an occasional dunking in icy water. Nobody owns them; they are a common-property resource, freely available at a monetary price of zero. But this fact does not make clams any less subject to economic analysis than goods with monetary price tags on them. A **demand schedule** exists for clamming. Like other demand schedules, it shows that more people will use more of the product at a low price than at a high one. Consequently, when the price is zero, as it was in Washington State clamming until the summer of 1979, the amount used will certainly be much more than at any positive price.

There also exists, hypothetically at least, a supply curve, although to discover positive prices we would have to envision private ownership of beaches and see how many clams would be offered by beach owners at various prices. The higher the price, the more would be offered. Presumably, if the price were right, the owner would incur costs of "cultivating" and protecting clam beds to increase their yield.

If a market situation existed, an equilibrium price and quantity could be established; but since a wide gap is inevitable between the amount demanded at zero price and the amount supplied at zero price, some device must ration the product. State authorities take on this task by setting daily catch limits and closing certain seasons to clamming. Regulations for the state of Washington first allowed noncommercial diggers to take 15 clams a day on any ocean beach from midnight to noon between March 16 and June 30. Unfortunately, these regulations were only a short-run solution. In the distant past, when the Pacific Coast was sparsely settled, no particular problem existed (in fact, no limit or season was set, since in those days, even at a zero price, the amount supplied exceeded the amount demanded).[1] But each year more and more people have more income for traveling to beaches and more leisure to devote to clamming. The result is that the demand keeps increasing, and each year happy clam hunters crowd

[1]By 1925, regulations did limit commercial harvesting of Washington razor clams to the months of March, April, and May. A well-trained clam digger can remove as much as half a ton of clams during one low tide. Given the state's sparse population, there was no reason then to restrict the season for noncommercial clam digging.

the minus-tide beaches. In Oregon, the clam-seeking camper sometimes faces traffic jams as much as a mile long.

It is possible to increase the supply of clams by opening new beaches or by having the State Fisheries Department cultivate more clams on existing beaches. But the increase can be only minimal once all the beaches have been made accessible. The ultimate result must inevitably be more crowding and fewer clams each year. It is not a happy prospect.

The clamming story is repeated over and over again for recreational activities, and the same analysis applies. In the case of wilderness areas, the supply is actually decreasing rather than merely remaining constant, as residential development takes place. All over the country, fishing, hunting, and camping sites are overcrowded, although these areas do have some potential for expansion of supply.

What is being done to improve the situation? A price is charged for fishing and hunting, in the form of license fees; and more recently, camping sites in parks are being "rented." In 1979, the Washington State legislature finally established a $2.50 resident (and $10 nonresident) clamming license. In each case, however, the rates have been set so far below the equilibrium price, which could balance quantities supplied with quantities demanded, that they are not even close to resolving the problem of overcrowding. And each year it gets worse. Anyone wishing to test this proposition need only visit Yellowstone or Yosemite National Park in the summer.

Constrast the case of clams with that of the oyster beds in the state of Washington, which were privately owned before the state restricted private ownership of tidal land. Those oyster beds were treated as an asset in which investment was made to improve the yield. In fact, the oysters were farmed just like any other agricultural commodity.

Perhaps a more spectacular contrast is between the north and south shores of Chesapeake Bay. On the north shore, the state of Maryland made the oyster beds a common-property resource; as would be expected where entry is unlimited, severe depletion has occurred. Moreover, it has not been worth-while to invest privately in improving the yield. In order to cut down on the harvest, the state has forced the use of archaic harvesting tools and archaic propulsion requirements (such as sail power). In contrast, the state of Virginia, on the south shore of the bay, allows private ownership of tidal lands. With 80 percent of the tidal land in private hands, owners have de-veloped the oyster beds into a thriving sustained enterprise. The average output per worker was 59 percent higher in Vir-ginia than in Maryland during the 25-year period 1945–1969.[2]

Why are we content with a zero, or now a nominal, price for clamming, fishing, or hunting? Apparently, the American people have long believed that such activities are a hereditary right, that they should be equally accessible to rich and poor alike, and that charging a fee favors the rich (which it certainly does). This argument prevails in the cases of clamming, fish-ing, and hunting, but not in the case of buying yachts and airplanes. The result is to artificially lower the monetary price for a particular publicly owned commodity—such as clams—but not for all commodities. In effect, the public policy is say-ing that income should not be a factor in people's ability to clam or to fish, but that it can be in buying golf clubs, TV sets, or airplanes. In effect, this is a policy of selective income redistribution.

As crowding, government rationing, and queuing be-come more and more severe in such nonpriced or underpriced activties, it becomes increasingly important to determine whether rationing by price or rationing by quantity restriction is the better method. One alternative is to eliminate the com-mon-property aspects of such resources, permitting them to be privately owned. Another is for the government to set a price that approximates a market price. The final alternative consists of a variety of rationing devices to restrict quantity

---

[2]Richard J. Agnello and Lawrence P. Donnelley, "Property Rights and Effi-ciency in the Oyster Industry," *Journal of Law and Economics*, vol. 18, no. 2 (October 1975), p. 531.

more and more rigidly. Whatever method is chosen, when all is said and done there's no such thing as a free clam.

DISCUSSION QUESTIONS

1. Clams are not really "free" goods, but rather goods sold at a low or zero price. Are there, in fact, any truly free goods in our society?
2. In the case of oysters, there seems to be no problem of overconsumption. What is the difference between the farming of clams and the farming of oysters?

22

Bubbleology: The Economics of Selling Pollution

Pollution, almost by definition, is undesirable. Most of us use the term so commonly it suggests we all know, without question, what it means. Yet there is an important sense in which "pollution is what pollution does." Consider, for example, ozone (O_3), an allotropic variety of oxygen. At upper levels of the atmosphere it is a naturally occurring element that plays an essential role in protecting life from the harmful effects of ultraviolet radiation. Without the ozone layer, skin cancer would likely become a leading cause of death, and spending a day at the beach would be as healthy as snuggling up to an open barrel of radioactive waste. At lower levels of the atmosphere, however, ozone occurs as a by-product of a chemical reaction between unburned hydrocarbons (as from petroleum products), nitrogen oxides, and sunlight.[1] In this form, it is an important component of smog, and breathing it can cause coughing, asthma attacks, chest pain, and possibly long-term lung-function impairment.

Consider also polychlorinated biphenyls (PCBs), molecules that exist only in manmade form. Because they are chemically quite stable, PCBs are useful in a variety of industrial applications, including insulation in large electrical transformers. Without PCBs, electricity generation would be more expensive, as would the thousands of other goods that depend on electricity for their production and distribution. Yet PCBs are also highly toxic; acute exposure (e.g., from ingestion) can result in rapid death. Chronic (long-term) exposure is suspected of causing some forms of cancer. Illegal dumping of PCBs into streams and lakes has caused massive fish kills, and is generally regarded as posing a threat to drinking water supplies. And since PCBs are chemically stable (i.e., they decompose very slowly), once they are released into the environment they remain a potential threat for generations to come.

As these examples suggest, the notion of pollution is highly sensitive to context. Even crude oil, so essential as a source of energy, can become pollution when it appears on the shores of Alaska's pristine beaches. Despite this fact, we shall assume in what follows that (1) we all know what pollution is when we see, smell, taste, or even read about it, and (2) holding other things constant, less of it is preferred to more.

There are numerous ways to reduce or avoid pollution. Laws can be passed banning production processes that emit pollutants into the air and water, or specifying minimum air- and water-quality levels or the maximum amount of pollution allowable. Firms would then be responsible for developing the technology and for paying the price to satisfy such standards.

---

[1]Ozone is also produced as a by-product of lightning strikes and other electrical discharges. Wherever and however it occurs, it has a distinctive metallic taste.

Or the law could specify the particular type of production technology to be used and the type of pollution-abatement equipment required in order to produce legally. Finally, subsidies could be paid to firms that reduce pollution emission, or taxes could be imposed on firms that engage in pollution emission.

No matter which methods are used to reduce pollution, costs will be incurred and problems will arise. For example, setting physical limits on the amount of pollution permitted would discourage firms from developing the technology that would limit pollution beyond those limits. The alternative of subsidizing firms that reduce pollution levels may seem a strange use of taxpayers' dollars. The latest "solution" to the air pollution problem—selling or trading the rights to pollute—may seem even stranger. Nonetheless, this approach is now being used in the majority of states. People like Stewart Rupp of Richmond, California, a partner in an environmental consulting firm, work as brokers, helping companies buy, sell, and trade the right to pollute.

To understand how this situation came about, we must understand the Federal Clean Air Act. This act was passed in 1969 in an attempt to force a reduction in pollution, particularly in metropolitan areas in the United States. Through rules and regulations of the Environmental Protection Agency (EPA), the Clean Air Act presents localities with specified permitted pollution levels. These so-called National Air Quality Standards must be met in most major metropolitan areas. However, in many of these areas air quality is already poor. Thus, a company that wishes to build a plant in such an area (referred to as a "nonattainment area," to distinguish it from an "attainment area," where the standards *are* met) is theoretically barred from doing so because of its detrimental impact on air quality. If the guidelines were strictly adhered to, it would mean no further industrial growth in many urban areas.

The EPA approved an "offset" policy to get around this problem. A company that wants to build a new plant in a non-attainment area is required to work out a somewhat larger reduction in pollution at some existing plant. The objective, then, is to produce a net overall improvement in air quality while still permitting development. For example, when Volkswagen wanted to build a plant in New Stanton, Pennsylvania, the state of Pennsylvania agreed to reduce pollutants from its highway-paving operations. This reduction would offset the Volkswagen plant's pollution.

One major problem with the offset policy involves the difficulty in finding an offset partner. In other words, each time a firm wants to build a new plant in an already polluted area, it must seek, on an individual basis, an offset partner that agrees to reduce pollution (usually after a payment from the first company). This is where the idea of brokering the right to pollute comes into play. This is where people like Stewart Rupp can go to work.

A company that closes a plant or installs improved pollution-abatement equipment can receive "emission credits" for its clean-up efforts that can be purchased by another firm. The firms involved negotiate the price. For example, the Times Mirror Company was able to complete a $120 million expansion of a paper-making plant near Portland, Oregon, after it purchased emission credits allowing it to add 150 tons of extra hydrocarbons to the atmosphere each year. A wood-coating plant and a dry-cleaning firm had gone out of business; they sold the necessary credits for $50,000 to the Times Mirror.

Using a broker to find firms that have emission credits to sell does not solve all the problems with the offset policy. Wisconsin has set up a computer system to track available credits for a nationwide trading system. In Illinois, the chamber of commerce and state environmental office established a clearinghouse to handle a market for the trading of pollution rights. More such centralized marketplaces are sure to spring up, since most states have already adopted regulations or issued permits allowing some form of air pollution offset.

Firms are also allowed to "bank" emission credits, i.e., cut pollution now in return for credits that can be sold or used in the future. One of the benefits of permitting the "banking" of pollution rights is that it increases the economic incentive to reduce pollution levels below those required by law. A firm that believes it could cheaply reduce pollutants further would find out that at some point another firm would pay it for such a reduction in order to build a new plant. Presumably, such a marketplace for the right to pollute would encourage further research and development in pollution-reduction techniques, an incentive that is missing when standards are set on an absolute physical basis.

Bubbles also play an important role in reducing pollution at a lower cost to society. A bubble is simply an imaginary airspace—typically occupied by an individual factory or plant—within which a firm may sum the emissions limits for individual sources of a pollutant and adjust the levels of control applied to different sources, as long as *total* emissions do not exceed the prescribed legal limit. Bubbles enable firms to use their knowledge of pollution-control costs to achieve efficiency gains without exceeding emissions limits, and to meet pollution standards that otherwise would not be feasible. (Bubbles generally are used only for different sources within the same firm. The operations of more than one firm can be and have been combined within a single bubble, however, with one of the firms selling some pollution rights to another firm within the bubble.) Although bubbles apply only to existing sources of pollution, a similar arrangement called *netting* applies to *new* sources of pollution. Thus, within a plant, a firm is allowed to create a new emissions source if it simultaneously reduces emissions from another source in the plant.

A variety of estimates have been made of the cost savings achieved as a result of programs that permit buying, selling, and trading of pollution rights among firms. While the savings from banking emissions credits are as yet relatively small, it has been estimated that bubbles and netting have combined to save more than $5 billion. The chief gains from offsets generally have not come in the form of readily estimated cost savings. Instead, offsets have yielded gains in the form of difficult-to-measure benefits of firms being able to locate in "nonattainment" areas, i.e., localities where existing air quality does not meet strict EPA standards. Importantly, it appears that the cost savings and other benefits of tradable emissions rights have been achieved without causing any overall net reduction in environmental quality.

Some observers have been disappointed that emissions-trading schemes have not produced even greater savings. There appear to be at least three reasons why greater gains have not been made. First, many environmentalists are vigorously opposed to the very *concept* of tradable emissions. As a result, the EPA has felt obligated to proceed slowly in developing new programs, to avoid a political backlash that might scuttle existing programs. Second, environmental regulators have periodically simply "wiped out" emissions credits that have been banked rather than used, on the grounds that doing so provides a convenient means of preventing future environmental damage. Not surprisingly, many firms have felt that a "use it or lose it" policy is the safest way to treat their credits. Finally, regardless of how great the cost savings of a plan might be, it has been difficult for firms to get plans approved unless they are able to convincingly demonstrate that *no* new environmental damage will occur. Unless obstacles such as these are removed, achieving environmental improvement at the lowest social cost is likely to remain a goal rather than an accomplishment.

DISCUSSION QUESTIONS

1. Does marketing the right to pollute mean that we are allowing too much destruction of our environment?
2. Who implicitly has property rights in the air if a pollution bank is set up and the right to pollute is sold to the highest bidder?

23

Crime and Punishment

The nation's prisons are full—and then some. The federal prison system, designed to hold 29,000 inmates, is operating at almost 200 percent of capacity.[1] The total of state prison populations is 550,000, up more than 75 percent since 1980 and 100,000 in excess of capacity. Many city and county detention facilities are packed with twice as many inmates as they were designed to house. Some correctional systems are so crowded they are under court order to release prisoners as fast as they admit new ones—regardless of the consequences.

---

[1]The "capacity" of a prison system is typically—though erroneously—referred to as though it were determined solely by immutable technological considerations. In fact, the economic capacity of a prison depends importantly on how luxuriously one wishes to accommodate the inmates—and thus is a matter of choice.

Today's crowded prisons are the result of two forces. First, the crime rate has been hovering at record levels since the mid-1970s. The chance that a household of four will be victimized by a serious crime in any given year is more than 20 percent—and rising.[2] Second, government authorities have become increasingly aware of the high costs that crimes impose on society, and have started toughening up law enforcement. The Federal Bureau of Investigation estimates that an average crime costs society about $2300. Since the typical professional criminal commits nearly 200 crimes a *year*, the annual costs imposed on society by such a person's crimes run $430,000. Many authorities now feel that the $25,000 to $40,000 a year it costs to keep a criminal in prison is beginning to look like a bargain. As a result, stepped-up law enforcement activities have doubled a criminal's chances of imprisonment over the last 15 years.[3]

Despite the high and rising cost of crime—made worse by the rapid spread of drug trafficking over the last decade— many taxpayers are reluctant to incur the costs of building more prisons. This attitude stems partly from the fact that new prisons are expensive: Prison construction costs run from $50,000 to $100,000 per bed, plus, of course, the operating costs of keeping prisoners on a daily basis. Importantly, however, taxpayer reluctance to foot the bill stems from a sense of uncertainty about whether punishment really deters crimes. Do tougher penalties really discourage people from committing crimes? What sort of penalties are most effective? Should criminals be fined, imprisoned, put on probation, or perhaps simply executed? Does capital punishment *really* deter people from committing murder? To begin to answer such questions, we clearly must have some notion of the economic relation-

[2]Serious crimes—called Part I crimes by the U.S. Department of Justice— include homicide, forcible rape, robbery, aggravated assault, burglary, larceny-theft, and motor vehicle theft.

[3]Despite this, a criminal is still significantly less likely to be imprisoned today than 30 years ago; between 1960 and 1975, the probability of being imprisoned for committing a crime fell from 6 percent to 2 percent.

ship between crime and punishment—or, perhaps more to the point, between punishment and crime.

There is one thing we can be sure of at the start: Uniformly heavy punishments for *all* crimes will lead to a larger number of *major* crimes. Let's look at the reasoning. All decisions are made on the margin. If an act of theft will be punished by the same fate, there is no marginal deterrence to murder. If a theft of $5 is met with a punishment of 10 years in jail and a theft of $50,000 incurs the same sentence, why not go all the way and steal $50,000? There is no marginal deterrence against committing the bigger theft.

A serious question is how our system of justice can establish penalties that are appropriate from a social point of view. To establish deterrents that are correct at the margin, we must observe empirically how criminals respond to changes in punishments. This leads us to the question of how people decide whether to commit a "crime." A theory needs to be established as to what determines the supply of criminal offenses.

Adam Smith, the founder of modern economics, once said:

> The affluence of the rich excites the indignation of the poor, who are often both driven by want, and prompted by envy, to invade his possessions. It is only under the shelter of the civil magistrate that the owner of that valuable property, which is acquired by the labour of many years, or perhaps by many successive generations, can sleep a single night in security. He is at all times surrounded by unknown enemies, whom, though he never provokes, he can never appease, and from whose injustice he can be protected only by the powerful arm of the civil magistrate continually held up to chastise it. The acquisition of valuable and extensive property, therefore, necessarily requires the establishment of civil government. Where there is no property, or at least none that exceeds the value of two or three days' labour, civil government is not so necessary.[4]

Thus, Smith concluded, in any society where one person has substantially more property than another, robberies will be

---

[4]Adam Smith, *The Wealth of Nations*, 1776.

committed. Following him, we can surmise that the individuals who engage in robberies are seeking income. We can also surmise that, before acting, a criminal might be expected to look at the anticipated returns and anticipated costs of criminal activity. These could then be compared with the net returns from legitimate activities. In other words, those engaging in crimes may be thought of as doing so on the basis of a cost/benefit analysis in which the benefits outweigh the costs. The benefits of the crime of robbery are clear: loot. The costs to the criminal would include, but not be limited to, apprehension by the police, conviction, and jail. The criminal's calculations are thus analogous to those made by an athlete when weighing the cost of possible serious injury against the benefits to be gained from participating in the sport.

If we view the supply of offenses in this manner, we can come up with methods by which society can lower the net expected rate of return for committing any illegal activity. That is, we can figure out how to reduce crime most effectively. Indeed, economists have applied this sort of reasoning to study empirically the impact of punishment on criminal activity. Time and again, they have found that: (1) increasing the probability that criminals will be detected, apprehended, and punished reduces the number of crimes committed; and (2) increasing the severity of the punishment has the same type of effect—the supply of crimes is reduced. One implication of these findings is that court-ordered early-release programs—which replace imprisonment with probation—can be expected to increase crime, particularly property crimes such as theft and burglary.

Can this theory be applied to a crime such as murder, and thus help us with a decision, pro or con, on capital punishment? Sociologists, psychologists, and others have numerous theories relating the number of murders committed to various psychological, sociological, and demographic variables. In general, they have stressed social and psychological factors as determinants of violent crime and have therefore felt that capital punishment would have no deterrent effect. Economists, on the other hand, have stressed a cost/benefit equation, which implies that capital punishment would deter violent crime.

We start with a commodity called the act of murder. If the act of murder is like any other commodity, the quantity "demanded" (by perpetrators, of course, not victims) will be negatively related to the relative price. But what is the price of murder? Ignoring all the sociological, psychological, and psychic costs of murder, we have to consider the probability of being caught and, after capture, the possible jail sentence or capital punishment that may be called for. We must also keep in mind, however, the *probability* that any particular penalty actually will be implemented. Thus, it would do little good to observe the difference in murder rates between states that have capital punishment and states that do not. Instead, we must assess the probability of a convicted murderer's actually being executed in those states that have capital punishment, and compare this probability with what happens in states that do not. In some states that allow capital punishment, for example, the probability of a convicted murderer's being executed is zero. We find, for example, that a charge of first-degree murder is often changed to a charge of second-degree murder if the penalty for murder is execution. In states that do not allow the death penalty, however, first-degree murder sentences are given more frequently. One manifestation of this is that "death-qualifying" juries—that is, juries consisting only of persons who do not oppose the death penalty—apparently are more likely to convict individuals of crimes for which the penalty is capital punishment.[5] Because these variations exist among states allowing capital punishment, it is necessary to look at the actual number of executions within a state, and not merely the laws, in order to establish whether capital punishment is actually a deterrent to murder.

[5]See, for example, the discussion of *Lockhard v. McCree* in "Death Penalty: A Barrier Falls," *Newsweek*, May 19, 1986.

Now, immediately critics of such cost/benefit analysis say that a typical murderer, either in a moment of unreasoned passion or when confronted with an unanticipated situation (for example, during an armed robbery), does not take into account the expected probability of going to the gas chamber. That is to say, murderers supposedly are not acting rationally when they murder. Is this a valid criticism of the economic model of the demand for murder? The answer is fundamentally an empirical issue, but even the logic of such an argument is suspect. Indeed, if one contends that the expected "price" of committing a murder has no effect on the quantity of murders, one is implicitly denying the law of demand, or stating that the price elasticity of the demand for murder is zero. One is also confusing the average murderer with the marginal murderer. All potential murderers do not have to be aware of or react to the change in the expected "price" of committing a murder for the economist's cost/benefit theory to be useful. If a sufficient number of marginal murderers act *as if* they were responding to the higher expected "price" of murdering, then the demand curve for murders by perpetrators will be downward sloping.

A few economists have actually used economic models to empirically study the demand for murder. One of the first statistical studies of significance is that by Isaac Erlich, published in 1975.[6] One of the variables he included was the objective conditional risk of being executed if caught and convicted of murder. Erlich found that a 15 percent increase in the chance of being executed would reduce the number of murders by about 1 percent. The implication of these results, given the number of murders and executions in the period covered by the study (1935–1969), is striking. The implied tradeoff between murders and executions was about 7 or 8 to 1. "Put differently, an additional execution per year over the period of

[6]Isaac Erlich, "The Deterrent Effect of Capital Punishment: A Question of Life and Death," *The American Economic Review*, Vol. 65, no. 3 (June 1975).

time in question may have resulted, on average, in 7 or 8 fewer murders."[7]

The deterrent effect of capital punishment on the crime of murder was more recently also analyzed by economist Stephen Layson, whose findings are even more suggestive. Layson concluded that every execution of a convicted murderer deters, on average, 18 other murders that would have occurred without it. He also studied the relationship between arrests and convictions of murderers and the murder rate. He found that a 1 percent increase in the arrest rate for murder would lead to 250 fewer murders per year and that a 1 percent increase in murder convictions would deter about 105 murders.[8]

As might be expected, these findings are highly controversial and have led to a debate that still goes on. Critics have stressed, for example, the tenuous statistical basis of Erlich's findings.[9] While the argument over capital punishment continues, the evidence that crime rates in general appear to vary inversely with estimates of penalties, probabilities of conviction, and legal opportunities has received substantial support.[10] Yet the arrest rate for murders is 75 percent; only 38 percent of all murders result in a conviction, and 1 percent of murders result in an execution. It is perhaps not too hard to understand why 75 percent of Americans now favor the death penalty.

One final note. In the case of capital punishment, or any other punishment, deterrence requires that the penalty must

[7]Ibid., p. 414.

[8]Stephen K. Layson, "Homicide and Sentence: A Reexamination of the United States Time-series Evidence," *Southern Economic Journal*, vol. 52 (July 1985), pp. 68–89. For an evaluation of Layson's conclusions, see Ernest Van Den Haag, "Death and Deterrence," *National Review* (March 14, 1986), p. 16.

[9]Peter Parsell and John R. Taylor, "The Deterrent Effect of Capital Punishment: Another View," *The American Economic Review*, vol. 67, no. 3 (June 1977), pp. 445–451.

[10]Gary Becker and William Landes, editors, *Essays in the Economics of Crime and Punishment* (New York: Columbia University Press, 1974).

be believed to fall on the guilty parties rather than to apply randomly. History tells us that under the emperors, executions in China were frequent. However, the emperors were not always so diligent about executing the right person. This system of "punishment" does little good for society in terms of combating crime, not to mention the loss suffered by the innocent victim and his or her family due to perverted justice.

DISCUSSION QUESTIONS

1. The analysis just presented seems to make the assumption that criminals act rationally. Does the fact that they do not necessarily do so negate our analysis?
2. In many cases, murder is committed among people who know each other. Does this mean that raising the price the murderer has to pay will not affect the quantity of murder demanded by perpetrators?

Part Five

Political Economy

INTRODUCTION

By now, you are certainly aware that many issues in our society have an economic basis. No matter what the economics of an issue may be, it probably has a political side, too. In fact, the subject matter of political economy is how the body politic decides on the allocation of resources. For the most part, political economy has as its basis different groups of individuals attempting to improve their economic position. Typically, a successful attempt by one group means that another group will suffer a deterioration in its economic position. Otherwise stated, the subject matter of political economy often involves a transfer of wealth among groups in society.

All the issues in this part are political in nature. In Chapter 24 we see how the politics of local government has effectively created an enormous increase in the market price for existing housing. In the chapters on ecology and government programs, the explicit issue of income distribution is examined, and it is shown that many programs designed to improve the environment and help disadvantaged groups in fact end up improving the economic status of the middle classes and the well-to-do. An economic analysis of poverty suggests the pervasive and sometimes perverse economics of politics. Examining the issue of educational choice, we learn that those having the most to lose by experimenting with choice are administrators and tenured instructors of relatively low quality who work in the public school systems. They, of course, will use their political clout, principally in the form of lobbying, to prevent a wholesale switch from our current educational system to one utilizing more freedom of choice. Finally, the air pollution caused by smokers is looked at as a classic case of a negative externality, where the cost of smoking also falls on nonsmokers breathing smoke-filled air.

Although politics plays a part in so many issues in our society, understanding the economic basis of political decisions can help one separate the reality from the rhetoric.

24

Killing the American Dream: Government Regulation and the High Price of Houses

Ara K. Hovnanian builds houses—*lots* of houses. In fact, his firm builds about 2300 houses a *year* up and down the east coast of the United States. Many of the houses Mr. Hovnanian builds are two- and three-bedroom "starter homes," but he also does a brisk business in the classic four-bedroom houses that many middle-income Americans either own or dream of owning. Mr. Hovnanian figures he can build a four-bedroom house in North Carolina for about $95,000. Building the same house in New Jersey costs him a minimum of $230,000. About 40 percent of the higher cost of the house in New Jersey is due to higher land prices in that populous state. The rest—some $80,000 *per house*—is a result of the welter of government regulations New Jersey has imposed on new home construction.

Spurred by a concern that New Jersey may be getting *too* populous, the state and local governments there have erected a maze of regulatory hurdles that has driven the costs and delays of building new homes to staggering levels. Obtaining approval to build a new house in North Carolina takes three to four months, start to finish. In New Jersey, the process of obtaining permit reviews, waging zoning battles, and fighting lawsuits by the owners of existing houses takes four *years*. Hovnanian, for example, employs 16 full-time lawyers just to get permission to build his houses. The result is higher costs, fewer new homes, and some hefty **capital gains** for the owners of existing homes.

New Jersey is not the only, nor even the first, state in which existing residents have used government regulations to keep newcomers out and house prices high. Beginning 20 years ago, Californians, having decided that too many people wanted to live in the Golden State, undertook to slow the state's rapid population growth. In Santa Barbara, for example, voters (many of them owners of existing houses) imposed a "water moratorium": New hookups to the county's water system were sharply curtailed, and in some areas actually *banned*. The result was a reduction in the number of new houses that could be built. The state's ongoing population growth was increasing the demand for houses, of course, which tended to push house prices up. Ordinarily, the rise in house prices would have spurred new building, which in turn would have dampened the price hikes. In Santa Barbara, however, the water moratorium virtually eliminated the construction of new homes. People wishing to move to the county had to buy *existing* houses—whose prices promptly skyrocketed. Measured in terms of today's dollars, house prices in Santa Barbara soared from $113,830 in 1972 to $235,630 in 1979. Of this amount, $36,500—nearly 30 percent—was due *solely* to the water moratorium.

The sharp reduction in new home construction in Santa Barbara, combined with the resultant run-up in the prices of existing houses, created a housing "crisis" in the county. New entrants to the area, and many low-income residents hoping to own a home, could no longer find "affordable" housing.

Over the last decade, governments in most other states have tried variants of the Santa Barbara plan for controlling unwanted growth. Time and again, the resulting reduction in the supply of homes has created housing "crises" and "shortages of affordable housing," especially for low- and middle-income buyers.

Appealing to the importance of preserving the "character" of their communities, a host of cities and counties across the country have fortified and extended zoning and land-use regulations to inhibit growth. While originally intended to impose sensible order on development, many ordinances now serve as barriers to all but the most expensive new housing. In Phoenix, for example, regulations mandate that most new homes be built with Spanish tile roofs instead of the cheaper asphalt shingling common throughout most of the United States. This little touch adds up to $6000 to the price new home-buyers must pay.

Back in New Jersey, when one developer began planning a 3300-unit condominium development in Secaucus, it was estimated the units would sell for $130,000. After six years of bureaucratic delays, the anticipated price had risen to $240,000. Originally, the firm estimated that 35 percent of area families would find the prices of its condos affordable. It now believes that only 18 percent of local families can afford the units. The developer, by the way, has yet to break ground on the project.

Communities interested in forestalling growth quickly realized that, since new houses require land on which to build them, by controlling the amount of usable land, they could control the amount of new construction. Thus, even as prices for raw land were rising over time, many communities stuck with—or tightened—tough zoning regulations that determine how many houses can be built on how much land. Since raw-land prices are the fastest-growing component of new home costs, the most effective way for builders to keep house prices down is to increase the number of units built on a site. But this requires variances from the zoning regulations.

Builders quickly found that any application for a variance was likely to be met with vigorous—and effective—opposition from the owners of existing homes. Indeed, as one observer has put it, existing homeowners have been so effective in their opposition to growth that "angry neighbors have become the fourth branch of government."

Communities in 31 states also now charge "impact fees"—thinly disguised property taxes that apply to new—but not existing—homes. In theory, such fees make developers pay for the added costs their projects impose on municipal services. When applied to services such as sewers, street lights, and even police protection, such fees help ensure efficient resource allocation.[1] But many cities are imposing impact fees to finance local "wish lists," such as new parks, senior citizen centers, and swimming pools—making new homebuyers pay for services that largely will be consumed by existing residents. In Los Angeles County, where explicit property taxes are limited by state law, impact fees have soared from $3000 to $22,000 per new house over the last 10 years. In effect, the impact fees act as taxes on new home construction, thus reducing supply and driving prices up.

The proliferation of permit reviews, fees, and density limitations has had some striking effects: Builders are switching to more luxurious, up-scale houses, leaving middle- and low-income buyers behind. The reason, as one builder puts it, is quite simple: "You have the same fixed overhead whether you build a $50,000 house or a $300,000 one, but it makes up a far smaller proportion of the selling price of the expensive home." In many areas where the regulations and fees add 25 percent to 30 percent to the cost of a new house, the addition of more luxury features can easily hike the price further by a comparable amount. Density limitations on the number of

---

[1]If new builders did not pay for the costs they imposed on existing residents, they would build more than the efficient number of new houses, because existing homeowners effectively would be subsidizing new home construction.

houses per acre are also gobbling up land in the few remaining close-in tracts around many cities. The vanishing land, combined with inflated house prices, are pushing new buyers farther and farther into the hinterland. Commuting distances of 75 and even 100 miles are becoming commonplace in both southern and northern California.

Traditionally, Americans have been upwardly mobile in their living accommodations. After five years or so in a "starter home," owners have used their accumulated equity to move up to larger homes, where their children are raised. This opens up the starter homes to apartment dwellers who want to enter the chain of home ownership. Soaring prices at the middle- and upper-price levels, however, have drastically slowed and sometimes halted this process of "filtering." When the starter homes aren't built, or don't open up, apartment dwellers stay put, driving rents up. This pushes people at the bottom end of the ladder into horribly cramped accommodations or even out into the streets. Indeed, many observers now believe that regulation-inflated house prices have contributed significantly to the rise in the number of homeless persons over the last decade.[2]

The growth phobia of local governments has also spawned the emergence of new slums—populated with houses in the $400,000 price range! New immigrant families, particularly in California, find themselves unable to afford any of the available houses—unless they "load up" the houses with two, three, or even more families. In many affluent Los Angeles County neighborhoods, it is not unusual to see campers parked in front of garages, attached to the main house with a heavy-duty extension cord. One family lives in the camper, drawing electricity from the house, which itself is occupied by two more families. A fourth family inhabits the garage. Some families have even resorted to "hot-bunking," occupying the house in shifts. While the members of one fam-

---

[2]For an additional force acting to raise the number of homeless, see Chapter 15.

ily work or go to school, another family sleeps and cooks; then they switch activities. Loading-up and hot-bunking illustrate vividly some of the many ways people manage to consume less of a good (housing services) when its price rises. All of this is usually in violation of zoning codes, of course, but for many it's either ignore the law or give up the American dream.

Some communities are beginning to recognize the full consequences of their no-growth policies, and thus have started to change the way they do business. In Portland, for example, the city has become more inclined to grant variances from its strict density-limitation rules. By permitting nearly ten homes instead of just four to be built on an acre of land, Portland has found that developers can cut the price of moderate-income housing by as much as 25 percent. Similar flexibility in the application of zoning regulations has permitted a modest proliferation of stylish, low-income homes on the outskirts of San Francisco. Interestingly, communities that have tried to work with developers, rather than against them, have found they can still plan their growth, even while letting more people enjoy the American dream. Until more communities get the message, however, one fact seems certain: Mr. Hovnanian's burgeoning staff of lawyers will have enough work to keep them busy for a long time to come.

DISCUSSION QUESTIONS

1. Does the difference in new-house prices between communities that limit growth and those that do not limit growth accurately reflect the impact of such limitations on the cost of houses of a given quality?
2. How might "impact fees" on *new* houses affect decisions of the owners of *existing* houses to engage in home improvements?

25

Ecology and Income Distribution

Most of us don't even think about it, but for residents of areas where there are scenic vistas, there are few more unsightly aspects of the urban environment than the jungle of poles and overhead wires that foul the typical cityscape. When we extend the term *pollution* to include visual pollution, overhead wires are a prime candidate for inclusion in this category. The solution is to place the wires underground, and this process is going on in many cities around the United States.

Often, the relocation of arterial wiring is paid for by a general utility rate increase; but in residential areas, it is not uncommon for the citizens of an area who want this change to form a Local Improvement District, develop a plan, and submit it to the appropriate body for approval. Usually the utility

company pays part of the cost, and each lot owner pays a pro-
portionate share of the rest. (In Seattle, for example, owners
and utilities have split the cost approximately 50–50.) Placing
wires underground in an already developed residential area is
expensive, with the total amounting to several thousand dollars per lot. It is not surprising that owner/utility cost sharing
has tended to restrict most underground wiring to higher-
income areas. However, since the share paid for by the utility
company comes from the total revenue received from everyone's rates, while benefits accrue to the upper-income groups,
such projects produce a redistribution of income from poor
to rich.

Two other options exist. We could insist that the lot
owner pay the entire cost of placing wiring underground, in
which case there would be no redistribution but also, probably, very little underground wiring. Or we could let the utility
company raise rates sufficiently to bury the wiring of the
whole city, in which case everyone would pay. At a public
hearing on the subject in Seattle several years ago, the head of
the local utility company testified that such a program stretch-
ing over a 10-year period would necessitate a doubling of electricity rates. A rate increase bears more heavily on the poor
because the percentage of their income that goes for electricity
is typically greater than the percentage for the rich. Thus the
consequence is again to impose a greater relative burden on
the poor than the rich. Is the case of underground wiring different in its effects on income redistribution from other solutions to environmental problems?

Before we attempt to answer this difficult question, we
reiterate a fact of which all readers should now be well aware.
Every action has a cost. That is, every action involves some
opportunity cost, whether or not this cost is explicitly stated or
even understood by those incurring it. Since our world is one
of limited resources, it is also a world of trade-offs. In the un-
derground-wiring example, we can pay higher electric rates
(or smaller amounts of income to spend on other things) in
return for beauty (no overhead wires). Beauty does not come

to us free of charge. When it is realized that every alternative course of action involves certain sets of costs, then it is time to ask who will bear the costs. We have already seen what happened in one case. We can now discuss others.

Many citizens are attempting to have forest areas preserved as pure wilderness, arguing that we should preserve as much of our *natural* ecology (as opposed to that made by humans) as possible. Preserving wilderness areas involves costs and benefits. The costs include less forest area for other purposes, such as vehicular camping grounds and logging. Who bears these costs? People who like to camp in trailers (but not backpack) in the first case, and people who buy houses and other wood products[1] in the second.

Although the reader can easily understand the first case, the second may not be so obvious. Look at it this way. When fewer forest areas are used for logging, the supply of lumber is smaller than it would be otherwise.[2] With any given demand (schedule) the price of lumber therefore will be higher than otherwise, and houses will be more expensive.[3]

Now for the benefits. Wilderness-area preservation offers benefits to those who like backpacking in the preserved area and to those who can enjoy fishing and hunting there. Benefits are also bestowed on those who do not themselves backpack, hunt, or fish but who would pay to keep the wilderness for their children.

To determine what effect saving a natural ecology area has on the distribution of income, broadly defined, we have therefore tried to discover, as always, who bears the costs and who obtains the benefits. This is usually an empirical question, which can be answered only by examining relevant data. From limited studies that have been done, we can make a ten-

---

[1]Or wood-product substitutes, for that matter.

[2]The supply schedule is farther to the left.

[3]The same is also true for nonwood houses. If the price of wood houses is higher than otherwise, more people will substitute nonwood houses—and their price will be bid up (their demand schedule shifts outward to the right).

tative conclusion about wilderness preservation: It has been found that backpackers are, in general, well educated and earn considerably more than the average. Thus the gains from wilderness preservation go to middle- and upper-income groups. As for who bears the costs, we know that vehicular campers (those with trailers, camper-trucks, and the like) are, on the average, less well educated than backpackers and earn considerably less. Hence, wilderness preservation implies fewer recreation facilities used by lower-income people in favor of those used by higher-income people.

As for the increased price of housing resulting from less lumber, we know that the poor will suffer more than the rich, because housing expenditures are a larger fraction of the poor's budget.

We can easily take other examples. Question: Should the level of a dam be raised to provide more hydroelectric power, or should the virgin timber area around it be left a wilderness area for backpackers? As economists, we cannot answer this question; we can merely point out all of the costs and benefits associated with two (or more) alternatives. In this example, the costs (in ecological terms) of raising the dam level would be borne largely by actual and potential backpackers. The benefits would be lower electricity rates or the saving of resources that would have been needed to develop an alternative source of energy supply. If electricity payments represent a larger fraction of the income of the poor than the rich, raising the level of the dam will tend to redistribute income from the rich to the poor.

There is, of course, a way of preserving our ecology without redistributing income.[4] The government could institute user charges for such things as wilderness areas and hunting preserves, setting them to cover the opportunity cost of the resources being used. The total receipts collected could then be redistributed in a manner that would compensate those bearing the costs. Such schemes are only occasionally used by

---

[4]But not without redistributing the use of resources.

governments, possibly because it is costly to determine exactly how much costs and benefits accrue to particular people. And so, preserving our ecology almost always involves redistributing income.

DISCUSSION QUESTIONS

1. Why aren't user charges imposed more often?
2. What would be the redistribution consequences of installing air bags in all new automobiles?

26

Waging War on Poverty

In 1965, the poorest 20 percent of the people in the United States earned about 5 percent of the money income in this country. Today, after a quarter-century of government efforts to relieve poverty, the bottom 20 percent *still* earns about 5 percent of money income. More than 30 million Americans lived in poverty 25 years ago; more than 30 million U.S. citizens *today* live in poverty, despite the expenditure of hundreds of billions of dollars in aid for the poor. Are America's efforts to aid the poor winning the war on poverty? Or are these efforts simply shifting the field of battle?

If we are to answer such questions, we must begin by getting the facts straight. First, even though the absolute *number* of Americans living in poverty has not diminished appreciably over the past 25 years, population growth has brought a reduction in the *proportion* of Americans who are impoverished. As conventionally measured, more than 17 percent of Americans lived in poverty in 1965; today only about 13 percent of the population is below the poverty line.

Second, traditional methods of measuring poverty may be misleading, because they focus solely on the *cash incomes* of individuals. In effect, government statisticians compute a "minimum adequate" budget for families of various sizes— the "poverty line"—and then determine how many people have cash incomes below this. Yet major components of the federal government's antipoverty efforts have come in the form of **in-kind transfers**—transfers of goods and services, rather than cash—such as Medicare, Medicaid, subsidized housing, food stamps, and school lunches. When the dollar value of these in-kind transfers is included in measures of *total* income, the standard of living of individuals at lower income levels is seen to have improved substantially over the years— relative to the "official numbers," and compared to the rest of society.

There remains disagreement over exactly how much of these in-kind transfers should be included in measures of the total income of recipients.[1] Nevertheless, most observers would agree that a reasonable inclusion shows that, over the last 25 years, the proportion of Americans living below the poverty line has been cut almost in *half*. Just as important, when in-kind transfers are taken into account, the share of total income going to the poorest 20 percent of the population has *more than doubled* since 1965. In short, the number of poor

---

[1]There are two reasons for this disagreement. First, a given dollar amount of in-kind transfers is generally less valuable than the same dollar amount of cash income, since cash offers the recipient a greater amount of choice in his or her consumption pattern. Second, medical care is an important in-kind transfer to the poor. Inclusion of all of the government's expenditures on Medicaid for the poor would imply that the sicker the poor got, the richer they would be, since Medicaid expenditures would be higher. Presumably, a correct measure would include only those expenses that the poor would have to incur if they were *not* poor, and thus had to pay for the medical care (or medical insurance) out of their own pockets.

individuals in this country has declined significantly, and those who are poor today are generally better off than the poor of 25 years ago. This conclusion is reinforced even if we look only at *cash* incomes: Since the mid-1960s, the inflation-adjusted cash income of people in the bottom 20 percent of the income distribution has risen about 20 percent; by contrast, the inflation-adjusted cash income of people in the *middle* of the income distribution has risen only about 10 percent.

The third important point to consider is that most Americans exhibit a great deal of **income mobility**—they have a tendency to move around in the distribution of income over time. The most important source of income mobility is the "life-cycle" pattern of earnings: New entrants to the work force tend to have lower incomes at first but usually can look forward to rising incomes as they gain experience on the job. Typically, annual earnings reach a maximum at about age 55. Since peak earnings occur well beyond the *median age* of the population (now about age 33), a "snapshot" of the current distribution of earnings will find most individuals "on the way up" toward a higher position in the income distribution. People who have low earnings now are likely, on average, to have *higher* earnings in the future.

Another major source of income mobility stems simply from luck. At any point in time, the income of high-income people is likely to be *abnormally high* (relative to what they can expect on average) due to recent good luck, e.g., they just won the state lottery or just received a long-awaited bonus. Conversely, the income of people who currently have low incomes is likely to be *abnormally low* due to recent bad luck, for example, they are laid up after an automobile accident or recently became temporarily unemployed. Over time, the effects of luck tend to average out across people. Accordingly, people with high income today will tend to have lower income in the future, while people with low income today will tend to have higher future income; equivalently, many people living below the poverty line are temporary rather than permanent residents.

The impact of the forces that produce income mobility are strikingly revealed in studies examining the incomes of individuals over time. For example, among the people who were in the top 20 percent of income earners at the beginning of the 1970s, less than *half* were in the top 20 percent by the end of the decade. Similarly, among the people who were in the bottom 20 percent income bracket at the beginning of the 1970s, almost half had moved out of that bracket by the end of the decade. Although exhaustive analyses of income data for the 1980s are not yet complete, the preliminary results show that *exactly* the same sort of income mobility occurred during that decade—and is likely to continue in the future.

Now that we have some notion that income numbers don't always mean what they seem, let's look at some of the other characteristics of the poor. In 1965, three groups were most "at risk" of being poor: blacks, the elderly, and women. The incidence of poverty among the elderly, for example, was more than *double* that of the rest of the population during the mid-1960s. Today, although many single elderly people remain poor, the poverty rate among the elderly is *lower* than for the rest of the population. As we saw in Chapter 14, an important reason for this reversal is the introduction of Medicare and the large increases in Social Security benefits that are two to five times what they and their employers contributed in payroll taxes, plus interest earned. The payback for Medicare beneficiaries is five to twenty times the payroll taxes today's elderly paid for this program. In essence, today's retirees are being subsidized heavily out of the payroll taxes levied on today's workers.

While blacks still earn less than whites on average, the income gap between the two races has narrowed markedly. In the early 1960s, black men earned only about 30 percent as much as whites; today this ratio is nearly 75 percent. Among women, the pay gap of blacks has risen from 54 percent of whites' pay to better than 97 percent. Similarly, the black middle class has expanded greatly, and shows every sign of continuing this expansion. Just in the last decade, for example, the number of black managers, professionals, technicians, and government officials has grown more than 50 percent. While there still remains a sizeable income gap between blacks and whites in America, substantial improvements in educational attainment and in race relations have helped many blacks reduce the gap significantly. This is not to say that the progress has been easy. The corporate bureaucracy remains predominately white, and many blacks believe that race still plays a role in evaluations of their job performance. As one black senior manager put it: "If you're a black boss, you're probably second-guessed more."

The economic position of women, too, has improved markedly during the last 25 years. Importantly, this has been due to a massive increase in the number of women entering the labor force; labor force participation by women has risen 50 percent since 1965. Although crude measures of wages show only a modest increase in women's pay relative to men's—with women now earning a bit under 75 percent of what men receive—many studies suggest that this apparent disparity is due largely to occupational choices made by women. Many females continue to choose career paths, such as primary and secondary education, that offer the greatest freedom in mixing family and work responsibilities. In jobs most nearly identical to those held by men, women's wages have risen relative to men's wages over the last 25 years, and women are gradually moving into positions that require a stronger commitment to long-term labor force attachment—and are being paid correspondingly higher wages as a result. Despite this, many women believe that far too often it is they—rather than their male counterparts—who have to make the toughest choices between family and work responsibilities.

The modest reduction in poverty over the past quarter-century has occurred largely because of the hard work and sheer determination of the individuals who have made the journey up the ladder of economic progress. Nevertheless, the upward migration of the poor of the '60s has been accompanied by substantial costs for other members of society. The federal government's efforts to facilitate this move has involved the expenditure of hundreds of *billions* of dollars—which in turn has meant sharply higher federal taxation.[2]

We noted in Chapter 14 that the taxes financing Social Security and Medicare—programs that have helped raise the living standards of the elderly—now take more than 15 percent of the paycheck of the typical worker. Expenditures on Medicaid, which finances hospital and doctor bills for the poor, are now running at $60 billion a year. Welfare expenditures, federal food programs for the needy, and housing subsidies for the poor add another $60 billion to the tab—all of which must ultimately be financed by taxes.

All government programs that transfer wealth among individuals affect people's decisions about how much—and what type of—work to do. Financing the programs requires higher taxes than would otherwise be the case. This reduces people's take-home pay, inducing some to work less, others to work less hard, and still others to refrain from working at all—or to join the "underground" economy, where their earnings are not recorded. The reduction in work effort means lower total income for society as a whole. The higher taxation also induces some people to take measures to avoid—or evade—those taxes. They concoct tax shelter schemes, whose purpose is not productive activity but simply tax avoidance; or they refrain from socially productive saving and investment because high tax rates lower their own private return from such activity. Again, the result is lower wealth for society as a whole. Finally, the cash and in-kind benefits offered by government transfer programs induce equally counterproductive behavior on the part of recipients. Some choose leisure rather than work, because the pay is almost as good; fathers leave their families to enable the latter to qualify for federal aid; and

[2]Another cost associated with the improved standard of living of the 1960s' poor—the creation of a *new* proletariat of the poor—is discussed in Chapter 27.

some people migrate to states offering higher welfare benefits. In each case, the incentives of the programs induce people to undertake actions that are in their own best interests but that reduce the total income available to society as a whole.

Estimating the magnitude of the "efficiency losses"— the economic cost to society—of our income-transfer programs is no easy task, and one sure to provoke controversy. Undaunted, economists have tried. One notable attempt is that by economists Edgar Browning and William Johnson. Focusing on the entire redistribution system—both taxes and transfers—they examined the effects of expanding it so as to transfer additional income from higher-income persons to the poor. They conclude that higher-income individuals sacrifice $350 for each additional $100 gained by the poor. The difference—70 percent of the amount given up by higher-income persons—is simply lost or wasted on the way to getting the $100 to the poor. Not everyone agrees with Browning's and Johnson's estimate. Even their most ardent critics, however, seem willing to admit that the losses are *at least* 35 percent of the amount taken from upper-income people. Considering that we now spend over $500 billion a *year* on income-transfer programs, the magnitude of the probable loss is truly staggering.

If such losses seem inconceivable, consider the following. Between 1973 and 1981, the federal government spent $55 billion on "job training" programs for the disadvantaged.[3] The avowed purpose of those programs was to improve the workplace skills of the poor, enabling them to earn higher wages, win better jobs, and avoid unemployment and welfare dependency. Over the last 15 years, the effects of these federal job training programs have been studied exhaustively, both by the government and by outside researchers. Almost uniformly, the conclusions reached have been the same: *Virtually the entire $55 billion was wasted.* Except for small numbers of young women who had no prior work experience, the partici-

[3]Under the auspices of the Comprehensive Employment and Training Administration (CETA) of the U.S. Department of Labor.

pants in the programs received almost nothing to enhance their labor market skills. As a result of the "job training" programs, they did not get better jobs, they did not earn higher wages, and they did not enjoy lower unemployment. Instead, they received ineffective training and "make-work" jobs while in the programs, and reverted to their prior poverty on leaving the programs. In 1981 the Reagan administration replaced the programs with the more promising Job Training Partnership Act (JTPA), but the $55 billion is gone forever.

Like most things in life, the reduction of poverty is not free. Ironically, one of the most significant costs of the government's effort to alleviate poverty is measurable not in dollars and cents, but in its impact on the structure of American families—particularly minority families. But that is a story best left for our next chapter.

DISCUSSION QUESTIONS

1. Why do most modern societies try to reduce poverty? Why don't they do so by simply passing a law requiring everybody to have the same income?
2. Which of the following possible in-kind transfers do you think raises the "true" income of recipients the most: (1) free golf lessons; (2) free transportation on public buses; or (3) free food?

27

The Changing Face of Poverty

Rachel and her children live in New York City. For five years their home there was one room in a basement: no kitchen, no toilet. When the city decided to move them to the Martinique Hotel—at a cost to the taxpayer of $1900 a *month*—it appeared as though things were looking up; at least they would have their own bathroom. But the Martinique was a "welfare hotel," and it, like the 41 other welfare hotels in New York City, was plagued with faulty wiring, box springs for beds, bureau drawers for cradles, rats, roaches, and—inoperable toilets. Now the city has closed the Martinique, and Rachel and her children reside in a temporary shelter, hoping that her welfare checks won't be delayed because they have moved.

While perhaps less fortunate than some, Rachel and her children typify today's poor in many respects. Among the 30 million or so people living below the poverty line in America, two groups predominate: youths (particularly minority youths) and members of single-parent families.[1] Regardless of their education, young people today earn less relative to older workers (aged 35–54) than they did 25 years ago. Among men aged 16–24 without a high school diploma, for example, the deterioration in relative earnings exceeds 10 percent. Among youths of both races, unemployment has increased drastically; the youth unemployment rate during the 1980s was double its level of the 1960s.

The deteriorating economic status of minority young-sters is exceeded only by that of families headed by women—families like Rachel's. Compared to two-parent families, the per-capita income of white mother-only families has fallen more than 10 percent since the sixties; among blacks, the deterioration is almost 20 percent. Moreover, the number of these families has increased markedly. In the mid-1960s, only about 10 percent of all families were headed by a single mother; today the figure exceeds 20 percent. More than *half* of all black families are now headed by women.

The enormous growth in the numbers and the dire financial condition of female-headed households is reflected in the rising relative poverty rate of children. Twenty-five years ago the poverty rate among children was not much above that of the rest of the population. Today, children are 50 percent more likely to live in poverty than is the rest of the population. Indeed, more than 40 percent of today's poor are children—mostly in families headed by women.

The modest reduction in poverty occurring over the past quarter-century (discussed in Chapter 26) has been accompanied by a major alteration in the identities of the poor. Indeed, the upward mobility of the poor of the '60s—black males, women, and the elderly—has been achieved only at

---

[1]A large proportion of elderly, widowed minorities is also below the poverty line. The small absolute number of such individuals, however, means they account for a very small percentage of today's poor—which does not, of course, improve the conditions under which they live.

substantial cost, not the least of which may have been the downward mobility of many of today's poor. Ironically, one of the most significant costs of the government's effort to alleviate poverty is measurable not in dollars and cents, but in its impact on the structure of American families, particularly minority families.

In general, poverty programs are "means-tested"; that is, if a person's or a family's income is judged by the government to be too high, eligibility for benefits is reduced or eliminated. For most families, the father is—or ordinarily would be—the primary source of income. If the family's income is above but close enough to the means-test level, there often is a financial incentive for the father to leave the family unit, so that his income is excluded when the family's eligibility is determined. And since eligibility is normally reviewed on a frequent basis, the departure is often permanent, save perhaps for occasional covert visits. Thus, the existence of welfare programs such as Aid to Families with Dependent Children (AFDC) actually *encourages* the breakup of the family unit: Either marriage never takes place, or the marriage is dissolved by separation or divorce, so that eligibility for federal benefits may be retained or achieved.

Many observers argue that the financial incentives of welfare are an important factor in the erosion of the two-parent family among blacks. Twenty-five years ago, for example, the marital status of black women and white women were quite similar: About two-thirds of each group was married. Today, although more than 60 percent of white women are married, only a bit over 40 percent of black women are married. Partly because of this decline in marriage among blacks, the incidence of illegitimate births among blacks is at record-high levels: More than 60 percent of all black children are born out of wedlock, a rate that is *four times* higher than observed among whites. This striking pattern may be encouraged by the very structure of AFDC payments. Since each additional child brings higher AFDC payments for the family, the welfare system provides a modest financial inducement for AFDC recipients to have more children. In short, many observers now believe that the government's efforts to relieve poverty have both altered the composition of the poor population *and* encouraged more poverty. Since the structure of the system discourages two-parent families among low-income individuals, and encourages the birth of additional children, we now have a population of the poor that is dominated by single-parent families and children.

As we noted in Chapter 3, another government policy—the minimum wage—has also fostered poverty among the young, particularly among minority youngsters. The minimum wage raises the cost of unskilled labor relative to skilled labor, and impinges particularly harshly on minority youths. Since the minimum wage creates a surplus of unskilled job applicants, some minority youngsters face discrimination in the process of deciding who shall be hired. Others, saddled with a lower-quality education, are prevented from offering to work for lower wages rather than go without jobs. In either event, current incomes of minority youths are reduced, and— perhaps most important—many of them are prevented from climbing onto the first rung of the economic ladder that leads to higher future incomes. In both the short run and the long run, the incidence of poverty among minorities is increased.

During the 1980s, a number of researchers attempted to estimate the number of youths denied jobs because of the minimum wage. The most plausible estimates put the number at about 400,000—most of them disadvantaged, minority youngsters. Perhaps most significant is that such estimates attempt to measure only the number of youngsters denied jobs *at a particular point in time*. The long-term damage of the minimum wage comes in its effects *over time*. Of the 400,000 or so youths denied jobs in 1985, for example, many thousands have given up looking for work and simply dropped out of the legitimate labor force. Denied a place on the first rung of the mainstream economic ladder, they failed to show up in the labor force statistics the next year or today. Some have turned to crime, others to drugs; many have found the combination appealing. The social toll grows every year.

The recognition that past and current government programs have actually helped create and shape the current population of the poor raises a troubling question: What changes in policy are appropriate in dealing with poverty? The Reagan administration tried to answer this question with some radical departures from past policy—in job training, housing, and welfare.

In 1981, the largely ineffective federal system of job training developed in the 1970s was abolished and replaced with the Job Training Partnership Act (JTPA). There were three key elements in this policy change: First, federal spending on job programs was cut better than 60 percent (to $3.3 billion a year, from its prior peak of $9 billion). Second, all of the money was to be spent on *training* workers rather than employing them in public-sector, make-work jobs—a practice that had been common during the 1970s. Finally, instead of day-to-day decisions about the use of funds being made in Washington, D.C., monies have been handed out to state and local governments to use as *they* see fit, as long as those uses are consistent with the overall training objectives of JTPA.

Despite the fact that JTPA was enacted early in the first Reagan administration, its full implementation took several years, and the jury is still out on its performance. An important element in the JTPA program has been the involvement of private businesses in the training process. Based on published reports, most businesses seem pleased—the training subsidies have enabled them to add new workers, and the relative lack of federal involvement in its administration has made the program much more attractive than its predecessors. Yet many critics argue that JTPA is too "results oriented," in the sense that it tries to recruit only the "cream of the crop," move them quickly through their training programs, and get them into jobs as soon as possible. Job placement rates for JTPA graduates appear to be higher than in any previous federal job training program, but these results largely may be due to the fact that the program has been more selective in picking its trainees. Only time—and careful scrutiny—will tell.

The Reagan administration also radically altered the federal government's approach to providing housing assistance for the poor. For many years, the standard strategy had focused chiefly on the construction of huge, high-density apartment complexes in deteriorating inner cities. Despite their high cost—about $70,000 per dwelling unit (in 1990 dollars)—the location and design of these public housing projects often turned them into "instant slums"—breeding grounds for crime and drugs. Reagan cut federal housing spending and largely eliminated the construction of such projects, moves that have been reaffirmed by President Bush. Today the emphasis is on providing housing subsidies for the poor—better than $12 billion worth a year—and letting *them* choose where to live.

An important ingredient in this approach consists of *housing vouchers*—government-provided subsidies that can be used by the poor to supplement their own resources in paying for housing. At an average annual cost of about $3500 per household helped, the vouchers pay the difference between 30 percent of the recipient's income and the "prevailing market rent," which nationally averages about $470 a month. Although the Reagan cuts in federal housing spending reduced the number of individuals receiving assistance, participation in the voucher program has been growing rapidly.

Critics of the voucher plan are dismayed that fewer poor individuals are now receiving housing assistance, arguing that some have become homeless as a result. Critics also note that the vouchers put added strain on the market for cheap rental housing. Proponents of the vouchers counter that vacancy rates for low-income housing are generally high throughout the country. Thus, except in cities like Boston and New York, where rent control laws keep apartment turnover low, nearly all voucher recipients find apartments within 60 days. Perhaps more to the point, proponents note, the benefits of vouchers spread far beyond their principal goal. Instead of warehousing the poor in urban ghettos, they allow recipients to decide where *they* want to live. By enabling black, inner-city welfare mothers to move to predominantly white suburbs, racial integration is enhanced, and the poor are able to live where better jobs are available.

On a far more limited scale, Reagan also experimented with reforming the welfare system. Principal among the approaches was the limited introduction of *workfare*, in which some AFDC recipients were required to work in return for a portion of their welfare payments. The program was limited to a handful of "pilot cities" under Reagan and has not progressed much further under President Bush. Proponents of workfare argue that an important component of training comes on the job; by inducing welfare mothers to enter the labor force, the prospects of their future workplace success—and higher incomes—is enhanced. Critics argue that most welfare mothers can't—or shouldn't—leave their children alone while working. Thus, they see workfare as little more than a thinly disguised attempt to drive impoverished single parents off the welfare rolls. To date, there is simply too little evidence on the workfare approach to assess its long-term implications.

In a variety of dimensions, then, the focus of the federal government over the past decade has been to eliminate programs that simply "throw money" at the problems of the poor and to reduce the intrusiveness of the federal bureaucracy in decision making. At the governmental level, this has meant increased reliance on activity and decision making by state and local authorities. At the individual level, it has meant added freedom—and responsibility—for the poor themselves. As yet, it is unclear whether the new focus will markedly reduce poverty—or perhaps simple create a new bottom tier of individuals unable to cope with the current rules of the game. As in many new ventures, there is hope. The housing voucher program, for example, made it possible for Mary Ann Hughes, a welfare mother of three, to move from a grim Chicago housing project to a home in the suburbs. "Now," she says, "instead of hearing gunshots, I hear birds singing." To some, at least, the new approaches sound like an improvement.

DISCUSSION QUESTIONS

1. How do the "rules of the game" help determine who will be poor and who will not?
2. Consider three alternative ways of helping poor people get better housing: (a) government subsidized housing that costs $3000 a year to provide; (b) a housing voucher worth $3000 a year toward rent on an apartment or a house; and (c) $3000 a year in cash. Which would you prefer if you were poor? On what grounds might the government decide which of these three programs to have?

28

Education and Choice:
The Economics of Schools

In 1974, East Harlem ranked 32nd among New York City's 32 community school districts. Only 15 percent of its students read at or above grade level. By 1989 this inner-city school district ranked 16th in New York City, and more than 65 percent of its students read at or above grade level. Moreover, the East Harlem district—located in one of the poorest areas of New York—today has a *waiting list* of teachers wishing to work there. What happened in East Harlem? A massive infusion of federal funds to promote educational reform? A multiyear grant from a major charitable foundation? Perhaps an influx of up-scale, yuppie parents demanding educational excellence? The answer: none of the above. What happened in East Harlem can be summarized by just one word: *choice.*

Back in 1974 the administrators of the East Harlem school district, faced with a school system that had nowhere to go but up, made a radical move: They decided to permit choice in their district. Teachers and schools were permitted to choose curricula and programs they thought would provide the best educational products, and students and parents were allowed to choose from among those products the ones best suited to their preferences and educational objectives. Along the way, mistakes were made and lessons learned. Some schools did a poor job, failed to attract "new customers," and have closed their doors. Other schools provided popular, effective programs that have been replicated successfully elsewhere in the district. Overall, the quality of education in East Harlem improved beyond even the most optimistic expectations of 1974. Indeed, the improvement was so great that the East Harlem educators decided to enter a new "market." The district had been administering education through the eighth grade only; in 1985 it assumed responsibility for a neighborhood high school with a graduation rate of 7 percent. Although the school accepts any student who wants to attend, its graduation rate now exceeds 90 percent, and almost all of its graduates go on to some kind of post-secondary education.

The freedom of choice offered schools, teachers, parents, and students in the East Harlem school district is unusual in public school systems today; but then so too is the success of East Harlem schools. In most school districts, the curriculum and course offerings for each grade level are decided on from "on high"—at the level of either the district or the state administrator. Once it is decided that, say, chemistry and biology, but not geology, are to be offered in high schools, then all high schools in the district typically must abide by that decision. Moreover, all individuals teaching, say, chemistry generally must follow the approved study plan and use the approved book for that course—without regard for the talents or interests of the particular teachers. The choices available to the "consumers" of education—students and their parents—are equally circumscribed. Once they have chosen a place to live, they are stuck with the particular set of schools, elementary through secondary, to which they are assigned by the district.

If, say, high school A offers advanced-placement chemistry and high school B does not, then students assigned to high school B simply will not have the option of taking advanced-placement chemistry in the public school system.

In important respects, then, each school district and each school within a district is much like a monopolist, albeit on a small scale. If the customers (students and their parents) of a district are dissatisfied with the quality, type, or amount of product being offered, they cannot—short of physically moving—choose to consume the services of another, nearby public school district. Similarly, if students or parents are dissatisfied with their assigned school within a district, they cannot choose a competing public school within the district.

It is true, of course, that parents and students can attempt to alter district or school policies by writing letters, voicing their opinions in school-board or PTA meetings, or engaging in political activities. Yet if they are in the minority—by even one vote—they are stuck with the preferences of the majority. It is also true that people can "vote with their feet" by relocating their residence to another school district or by utilizing the services of private schools. Yet such measures are extremely costly, and thus they generally are taken only by persons who are either extremely dissatisfied or extremely wealthy. Few rational people are willing to sustain the cost and inconvenience of selling one house and buying another simply to enjoy a school system that is a little better—particularly since they will have so little voice in the operation of the *new* school system once they have chosen it. And for those people opting for private schools, there is a double burden to bear: In addition to the bills for private school tuition, they must continue paying taxes to support the public school system they find unsatisfactory! All in all, then, public schools are largely insulated from competition.

This situation is in sharp contrast to the market for, say, magazines—which, like schools, are a source of knowledge and (for some) entertainment. Consider, for example, *Time* magazine, which is headquartered in Manhattan, a borough of New York City. Taxes are not levied on the residents of Manhattan to cover the costs of publishing *Time*, and one need not be a resident of Manhattan to read it; residents of Brooklyn, East Harlem, and even Honolulu are free to read it—should they choose to pay for it. If the owners of *Time* produce a high-quality product at a reasonable price, readership will grow and the owners of the magazine will get wealthy (which is, presumably, why the owners are in business). If the owners produce a shoddy product or charge a price that is too high, consumers can and will switch to any one of numerous competing news magazines, thereby reducing the wealth of the owners of *Time*. In either event, competition among magazines yields diversity of choice and the provision of high-quality products at reasonable prices.

We have already noted how the relative lack of competition among public schools restricts the choices available to parents and students. Many experts also believe that the monopolistic position of public schools has contributed to inferior primary and secondary education in the United States, relative to other comparable nations, and to a significant decline in educational quality in the United States over the past quarter-century.

It has long been recognized that when American students are exposed to educational systems in other industrialized nations, they are commonly at least a grade level behind the other students in those countries, even in standard subjects such as mathematics. Recent research has systematically confirmed this observation. One major study, for example, found that the *average* Japanese student outscores the top 5 percent of U.S. students enrolled in college-prep math courses. Other research has revealed that in chemistry and physics, advanced science students in U.S. high schools perform worse than their counterparts in almost all countries studied. And in biology, American students ranked dead last, behind such nations as Singapore and Thailand.

In part, the superior performance of foreign high school students is explained by the fact that many foreign nations place more emphasis on training at the primary and secondary school levels and less emphasis on college-level training. Nevertheless, many observers agree that the lack of competitive pressure among public school systems in this country has largely robbed U.S. schools of the incentive to excel. Even the president of the American Federation of Teachers has acknowledged the deficiency in American schools: "Only about 5 percent of our graduates leave high school prepared to do what is considered real college-level work. . . . The overwhelming majority of American students who go on to higher education will be learning in college what their European colleagues learned in high school or even junior high school."

There is also little doubt that the quality of education in American school systems has deteriorated over the past quarter-century. Between 1963 and 1980, scores on the widely used Scholastic Aptitude Test (SAT) plunged 90 points; in the decade since they have recovered only 14 points of that loss. Between 1972 and 1981 the number of high school seniors scoring above 600 (out of a possible 800) on the verbal portion of the SAT dropped 40 percent; even today this remains nearly 30 percent below the 1972 figure. Although scores on the mathematics portion of the SAT have held up somewhat better, this amounts to little more than stagnation in an area seriously requiring significant improvement. In 1988 the federally funded National Assessment of Educational Progress (NAEP) found that, despite supposed efforts at "educational reform" in this country, the previous decade had witnessed improvements in mathematics skills that were "confined primarily to lower-order skills." Indeed, the NAEP report concluded that only 6.4 percent of high school seniors have mastered "multi-step problem solving and algebra"—exactly the sort of skills essential to successful performance at the college level.[1]

---

[1]Consider, for example, the following question: "Which of the following is true of 87% of ten? (a) It is greater than 10. (b) It is less than 10. (c) It is equal to 10. (d) Can't tell." The NAEP report concluded that all high school seniors should be able to answer this question correctly. In fact, only 51 percent were able to do so.

What is to be done about the sad state of primary and secondary education in this country? Many observers argue that competition among schools, fostered by greater freedom of choice, is pivotal in any solution. The experiment of the East Harlem school district is one example of the power of choice in promoting excellence. On a much broader scale, a series of programs begun in the state of Minnesota are providing even more compelling evidence of the importance of choice.[2]

In 1985 the governor of Minnesota proposed that juniors and seniors in public schools in the state be permitted to receive all or part of their last two years of high school in colleges or vocational schools, with state monies following them from high school to pay their tuition, lab fees, and book fees. The governor also recommended that families be allowed to send their offspring to public schools outside their home districts, as long as the receiving districts had room and the movement did not harm desegregation efforts. Despite vigorous opposition to the proposals by the teachers' unions, school boards, and superintendents' groups, four laws allowing greater freedom of educational choice have been passed in Minnesota, and the results are encouraging.

Since 1985 more than 10,000 students have taken advantage of the program permitting them to take college courses while still in high school, and many of them have higher grade point averages in those courses than do the regular freshmen students. The program has attracted hundreds of students who had dropped out of high school due to boredom or frustration. Moreover, many participants are, because of the new program, the first in their families to attend college. As one of these students put it, the program "changed my sense of what was possible."

Just as important, the program has stimulated many high schools to improve their own programs. Between 1985 and 1989 the number of advanced-placement courses offered

[2]See Joe Nathan (ed.), *Public Schools by Choice* (Bloomington, Ind.: Meyer-Stone, 1989).

by Minnesota high schools quadrupled—*without* any new mandates or dollars targeted for this purpose. And more than 50 high schools have been spurred on to establish cooperative programs with colleges and universities that let them offer courses right in the high schools.

Under another Minnesota program, begun in 1987, students who don't succeed in one junior or senior high school are allowed to attend a school outside their district. Several thousand students have already taken advantage of this plan— about half of them school dropouts. Another law, passed in 1988, will eventually enable Minnesota students in all grades to attend school outside their districts, subject to space and racial balance considerations. Within less than a year of the law's passage, more than 3000 students had applied for transfers.

The East Harlem and Minnesota programs are just two examples showing that when choice among schools is permitted, the resulting competition improves the quality of education. Programs in other locales are reaffirming this conclusion: When students are given a choice of schools, graduation rates improve, student achievement increases, and parents are more involved and satisfied. Even teachers and school administrators—often initially fearful of the consequences of competition—are apparently finding that the opportunity to create new and distinctive programs offers rewards far outweighing the extra effort involved.

The famous professional golfer Arnold Palmer once remarked, "If you're not competing, you're dead." For America's moribund public school systems, the message from Minnesota and East Harlem seems to be the converse of this dictum: competition brings vitality. It is easy to imagine that today's students are hoping this message is being received as clearly as it is being transmitted.

DISCUSSION QUESTIONS

1. Who gains and who loses when there is more competition among public schools?

2. Some people have argued that we should institute educational vouchers that could be used by students to finance their education in *either* public schools or private schools of their choice. What are the advantages and disadvantages of such a scheme?

29

Income Distribution
and Government Programs

As is true in many countries, our government operates programs for helping sectors of the economy where aid seems to be needed. In most cases, the implicit aim of these programs is to effect a redistribution of income.

We noted in Chapter 27 that all programs to improve or maintain our environment involve both costs and benefits. This is true of any government program. If we are to understand the actual, as opposed to the avowed, redistributional aspects of any governmental policy, we must fully assess the range of costs and benefits. Also, we must determine empirically who bears these costs and benefits.

Let us examine the redistributional effects of the farm program. The avowed intent of this program is to maintain farmers' incomes at a level that society feels is acceptable (that is, not "too" low). The questions to be asked are: (1) Does the program fulfill that purpose, i.e., who reaps the benefits? (2) How is the program paid for, i.e., who incurs the costs?

To answer the first question: Those farmers who produce and sell the most crops will receive the most income from the government, since farm subsidies are geared to actual or potential farm output levels (see Chapter 4). In general, this means that benefits from the farm program are proportional to farmers' incomes, since those with larger farms usually have higher incomes. Because almost 90 percent of all agricultural crops marketed are produced by about 10 percent of U.S. farmers, it is evident that the farm program is not benefiting mid-sized and smaller farmers—as it was intended to do. Indeed, a recent study by the Deparment of Agriculture indicates that the vast majority of income and price support payments go to the largest and wealthiest farmers. And only 18 percent of farm-program payments go to the neediest farmers. It is the farmers in the latter group who are leaving the business of agriculture in droves for other income-producing alternatives. During the 1980s, nearly 50,000 farmers *per year* quit the business of farming because they could no longer meet their costs.

The farm program also tips the scales in favor of wealthy farmers in another way. This is because higher-income farmers have more access to knowledge of legal procedures that can help them maximize their benefits from the farm program. Currently, for example, farm-program regulations specify that no person can receive for any one crop more than $50,000 worth of a specific type of subsidy, called a deficiency payment. But the regulations allow a "person" to be a corporation, a partnership, or a trust—as well as an individual farmer. Technically, as long as any of these legal entities (1) has a legal interest in the land or crop, (2) participates in management, and (3) is liable for losses as well as profits, that entity is entitled to deficiency payments. In order to increase their payments from the government to more than this $50,000 maximum, many farmers have taken advantage of this rule and formed two or more legal entities within the same family. According to Agriculture Department officials, it is common to find farms splitting into 4 to 10 or more legal units over a period of years. In one case, a rice farm in California was divided up 56 ways—and received nearly $1.5 million in income subsidies.

The total value to farmers of the various government subsidies they receive has been running about $25 billion *annually* in recent years. Of this, about 80 percent, or $20 billion a year, is paid for by taxpayers. The remaining $5 billion a year is borne by consumers, chiefly in the form of higher food prices. We have already seen that the benefits of the subsidy programs go chiefly to middle- and upper-income farmers. Since middle- and upper-income taxpayers pay out a larger share of their income in taxes than do lower-income taxpayers, the taxation component of farm subsidies represents chiefly a redistribution of income from the nonfarming upper half of the income scale to the farming upper half of the income scale. As for the component borne by consumers, however, lower-income people tend to spend a larger proportion of their income on food than do middle- and upper-income people. In this regard, then, farm subsidies transfer income from lower-income individuals to middle- and upper-income farmers. Overall, farm subsidies tend to benefit the top half of the income distribution at the expense of the bottom half.

Turning now to our income tax system: Let us consider how certain tax deductions redistribute income. An individual paying off a home mortgage is allowed to deduct the interest payments from income when calculating taxable income. This is an incentive for home ownership, since buyers benefit by not having to apply their tax rate to that amount of income. Ms. A, whose annual mortgage interest payments equal $1000 and whose tax rate is 15 percent, will gain $150 in income that does not have to be handed over to the government. Splendid! But consider the case of Mr. B, who earns twice the salary of Ms. A, has double the house, and is in the 28 percent tax bracket. For the $2000 he paid out as interest this year, which he deducts from his income tax, he saves $560. The rich individual with a mortgaged home has benefited more than a less rich person in the same situation and far more than a poor individual whose tax rate is zero, or than anyone who has no mortgage payments on which to receive concessions.

This type of analysis can be applied to a host of issues. For example, you may recall that in Chapter 1 we considered the ways in which income is redistributed by laws that make prostitution and narcotics illegal. In both cases we can say that, since information is more costly for illegal goods and services, in general those who can afford to pay more (the wealthy) receive a "better" product than those who are poor.

In a markedly different vein, we saw that minimum-wage legislation also affects the distribution of income. When potential employees are prohibited by law from competing for jobs on the basis of lower wages, employers must use some other grounds for choosing among job applicants. In practice, many employers seem to prefer to hire middle- and upper-income whites rather than lower-income minorities when the law prohibits wage competition. Thus, minimum-wage legislation tends to redistribute income from low-income minorities to middle- and upper-income whites.

We can also recall the issue of rent control. If laws controlling rents are effective, they establish a price below the market-clearing price. Dealers in rent-controlled apartments therefore look for nonpecuniary returns when renting. Who is a better risk, a person who makes $30,000 a year or a person who works off and on for about $10,000 a year? Under rent control, will the landlord rent to a welfare recipient or to the daughter of a city council member? At the same rental price, the landlord will probably rent to the latter, since she is more likely to make her rent payments regularly.

All of these examples demonstrate the need to study the distribution of the costs and benefits of government programs and to decide whether they actually redistribute income in the intended direction. To the contrary, it appears that many policies tend to favor the rich at the expense of the less rich. Naturally, this conclusion must be examined anew for any prospective program.

DISCUSSION QUESTIONS

1. Discuss a government program that favors the poor.
2. On balance, what are the distributional consequences of federal government tax and expenditure programs?

30

Where There's Smoking, There's Fire

Thirty years ago smoking existed everywhere; indeed, it was something of a status symbol to smoke. Television ads and movies showed the heroes and heroines dangling cigarettes from their mouths. Since then, the image of the smoker has changed dramatically. Smokers are now condemned by many as self-indulgent, self-destructive polluters who are inconsiderate of the effect their smoke has on others nearby. Recent opinion polls show that nearly 90 percent of nonsmokers think that smokers should refrain from smoking when others are present. Yet polls show also that, while smokers may be self-indulgent and self-destructive, they are not all inconsiderate of others: more than 60 percent of smokers agree with the nonsmokers that smokers shouldn't inflict their smoke on third parties.

The beginning of this dramatic change in attitudes toward smoking can be dated from the 1964 Surgeon General's report, which made it clear that smoking is harmful to health. As the link between lung cancer and smoking became more firmly established, increasingly stern labels were required on cigarette packages to warn consumers of the health hazards caused by smoking. In recent years, the focus has been broadened to include the adverse health effects of smoking on "passive smokers," nonsmokers who are continually exposed to smoke-filled air either at home or in the workplace. One study showed that 5000 Americans die every year as a result of second-hand smoke, and a recent Japanese report concluded that wives of heavy smokers had an 80 percent higher risk of developing lung cancer than women married to nonsmokers. Heart disease has also been connected to passive smoking. The exact degree to which smoking physically harms nonsmokers, though, is still a debated question; vehement proponents of the rights of smokers can cite several scientific studies that have been unable to establish a relationship between "passive" smoking and significant harmful health effects. But there is no doubt that smoking can be irritating and obnoxious for the nonsmoker and that, whether they want to or not, nonsmokers are forced to breathe the polluted air created by smokers in numerous situations.

Smoking is a classic case of an externality, one for which it would be appropriate for the smoker to compensate the nonsmoker for the discomfort felt—according to the efficiency standards of the economist. Or, in the absence of compensation, the correct policy might be to impose rules and regulations that prevent the smoker from being able to irritate the nonsmoker. Why doesn't the federal government simply ban smoking? Ultimately, the issue becomes one of political economy, in which the interests of competing groups are balanced—often with peculiar results. What the government does with its left hand—the Surgeon General's Reports, which have resulted in a heavily subsidized publicity campaign to prevent smoking—is countered by its right hand—

the Department of Agriculture's subsidies to the tobacco industry. The approximately 500,000 growers of tobacco in the United States are prevented from competing by laws that restrict tobacco acreage and provide a prohibitive tax of 75 percent on all tobacco grown on unlicensed land. The result is large monopoly returns to those growers fortunate enough to have been in on the beginning of this subsidy (which started some four decades ago).

There's still more to the right hand of government. The low elasticity of demand for tobacco makes it an excellent source of tax revenue. Indeed, federal tax receipts from the sale of cigarettes now run about $5 billion a year, and this doesn't include receipts from import duties on tobacco and tobacco products. Clearly, some parts of the federal government feel they have a great deal to gain from the continued use of tobacco. So does the subsidized farmer in the American South, who is receiving direct returns from the monopoly granted to tobacco growing. And—it goes without saying—so, too, do the 50 million Americans who call themselves smokers, and who spend over $30 billion a year for tobacco products.

There is little doubt that if smoking were discovered for the first time today it would be put in the same class as cocaine, heroin, and other dangerous drugs, and be considered something that should be outlawed by society. But smoking became a national craze in an era when it was viewed as prestigious, and it still retains much of that aura for young people. And obviously smokers are voters, too, as are tobacco growers and the growing legions of antismokers. As a result, it is not surprising that the politics of smoking should lead to contradictory roles of government—where the left hand works to prohibit smoking and the right hand to promote it.

State and local governments provide an interesting illustration of the forces of political economy behind the seemingly contradictory behavior of the federal government. To date, 42 states and more than 400 local governments have enacted rules restricting smoking. Not surprisingly, these restrictions are more prevalent where tobacco is an unimportant part of the local economy. For example, in 1975 Minnesota became the first state to pass a comprehensive clean-indoor-air act. Virginia, by contrast, where tobacco is a $2.8-billion-a-year industry, recently passed legislation outlawing discrimination against smokers. (A half-dozen other states, predominantly in the Southeast, have similar legislation under consideration.) New York City, whose mayor had not smoked since 1952, not only passed stiff legislation that restricts smoking in public, but has also hired 70 smoke police to enforce the rules. Meanwhile, most cities and counties in tobacco states such as Kentucky, Virginia, and the Carolinas have steadfastly refused to seriously limit where smokers may light up.

Within the business community, more than half of all firms have restrictions on smoking at work. Some ban smoking on the job altogether, and roughly 6 percent of all firms refuse to hire smokers. At a few firms, smoking *off* the job is grounds for dismissal. Importantly, firms are cracking down on smokers because of the growing evidence that smoking reduces productivity and also raises firms' health insurance costs. Their policies also seem to be influenced, however, by the habits of top management: When the boss smokes, employee smoking is more likely to be tolerated. This fact alone suggests that additional workplace smoking restrictions are likely in the future. Over the past decade or so, white collar workers have been much more diligent in curbing their smoking appetites than have blue collar workers. Thus, it is estimated today that smoking among white collar workers is only *half* as prevalent as among blue collar workers.[1] As the smoke-

---

[1]This pattern is hardly surprising. White collar workers are, on average, better educated and thus more likely to be aware of the full range of hazards associated with smoking. They also tend to earn higher incomes; a 10 percent loss in output (and thus income) for a person capable of earning $100,000 a year when healthy is clearly more expensive than a 10 percent loss in output for a person who is worth, say, $20,000 a year at peak performance.

free yuppies of the '80s become the bosses of the '90s and beyond, cleaner air on the job is likely to follow.

As the smoke clears, there is a certain irony in the spreading restrictions against lighting up the "evil weed." For many years in this country, chewers of tobacco outnumbered smokers. Early in this century, however, social reformers, concerned about the spread of tuberculosis, launched a campaign to prohibit public spitting—an activity developed into an art form by tobacco chewers. Faced with a compelling community health problem, town after town imposed a ban on spitting. Unwilling to fight, Americans seeking a nicotine jolt thus made a large-scale switch to the "safer" alternative—cigarettes. So much for progress.

DISCUSSION QUESTIONS

1. Is there a similarity between the analysis of smoking and the analysis of the use of wilderness areas by motorcycle riders?
2. How would you compare the problem of air pollution created by smokers to that of pollution created by industrial plants?

Glossary of Terms

Acreage restriction program: Government program under which farmers agree to hold some of their acreage out of production in return for some compensation from the government. The purpose is to reduce the supply of the covered crops, driving their prices, and thus farmers' incomes, up.

Bond: An interest-bearing certificate issued by a government or a corporation. This type of security represents debt.

Capital: All manufactured resources, including buildings, machines, and improvements to land.

Capital gain: The positive difference between the purchase price and the sale price of an asset. If a share of stock is bought for $5 and then sold for $15, the capital gain is $10.

Cartel: A group of independent industrial corporations, usually on an international scale, that agree to restrict trade, to their mutual benefit.

Collateral: Any assets a borrower agrees to forfeit in the event a debt is not repaid as agreed.

Common property: Property that is owned by everyone and therefore owned by no one. Examples of common-property resources that have historically been owned in common are air and water.

Common stock: A security that indicates the real ownership in a corporation. A common stock is not a legal obligation for the firm and does not have a maturity. It has the last claim on dividends each year and on assets in the event of the firm's liquidation.

Competition: Rivalry among buyers and sellers of outputs, or among buyers and sellers of inputs.

Complementary goods: Two goods are considered to be complementary if a change in the price of one causes an opposite shift in the demand for the other. For example, if the price of tennis rackets goes up, the demand for tennis balls will fall; if the price of tennis rackets goes down, the demand for tennis balls will increase.

Constant quality unit: A unit of average, or standard, quality by which all units are measured.

Consumer Price Index: A statistical measure that is a weighted average of prices of a specified set of goods and services purchased by wage earners in urban areas.

Deficit: The negative difference between inflows and outflows, or, more specifically, between income and expenditures; as applied to government, the term is *government budget deficit*.

Demand curve: A graphic representation of the demand schedule. A negatively sloped line showing the inverse relationship between the price and the quantity demanded.

Demand schedule: A set of number pairs showing various possible prices and the quantities demanded at each price. This schedule shows the rate of planned purchases per time period at different prices of the good.

Discounting: A method by which account is taken of the lower value of a dollar in the future compared to a dollar in hand today. Discounting is necessary, even after adjustment for inflation, because of the tradeoff between having more goods tomorrow if we consume less today.

Distribution of income: The way income is distributed among the population. For example, a perfectly equal distribution of income would result in the lowest 20 percent of income earners receiving 20 percent of national income and the top 20 percent also receiving 20 percent of national income. The middle 60 percent of income earners would receive 60 percent of national income.

Economic good: Any good or service that is scarce.

Economies of scale: Savings that result when output increases lead to decreases in long-run average costs.

Elastic demand: A characteristic of a demand curve in which a given percentage change in price will result in a larger percentage change in quantity demanded, in the opposite direction. Total revenues and price are inversely related in the elastic portion of the demand curve.

Elasticity of demand: The degree to which buyers will be sensitive to and respond to a change in price.

Equilibrium, or market-clearing, price: The price that clears the market where there is no excess quantity demanded or supplied. The price at which the demand curve intersects the supply curve.

Expansion: A business fluctuation in which overall business activity is rising at a more rapid rate than previously, or at a more rapid rate than the overall historical trend in a particular country.

Externalities: A situation in which a benefit or a cost associated with an economic activity spills over to third parties. Pollution is a negative spillover, or externality.

Free good: Any good or service available in quantities larger than are desired at a zero price.

Generic drugs: Drugs marketed under the generic name of the drug rather than under a brand name for the same drug. As long as a pharmaceutical firm holds a patent for a brand-named drug, that drug cannot be sold generically.

Income effect: The change in purchasing power that occurs when the price of a purchased good changes, other things being held constant.

Income elasticity of demand: The percentage change in the quantity demanded divided by the percentage change in money income; the responsiveness of the quantity demanded to changes in income.

Income mobility: The tendency of individuals' incomes to change relative to the incomes of other people over time. It is most commonly caused by the fact that individuals' incomes tend to grow more rapidly than average up to age 40 or 45, then grow more slowly than average up to age 55, and then begin to decline.

Inelastic demand: A characteristic of a demand curve in which a given change in price will result in a less-than-proportionate change in the quantity demanded, in the opposite direction. Total revenue and price are directly related in the inelastic region of the demand curve.

Inflation: A sustained rise over time in the weighted average of all prices.

In-kind transfers: Items of value other than money that are given to individuals by the government, e.g., medical care, housing, and food.

Inside information: Any information that is available only to a few people, such as officers of a corporation.

Investment: The sum of fixed investment and inventory investment. Any addition to the future productive capacity of the economy.

Labor: Productive contributions of individuals who work, involving both thinking and doing.

Law of demand: A law that states that the quantity demanded and price are inversely related—more is bought at a lower price, less at a higher price (other things being equal).

Law of supply: A law that states that a direct relationship exists between price and the quantity supplied (other things being equal).

Liability: Anything that is owed.

Marginal costs: The change in total costs due to a change in one unit of production.

Marginal tax rate: The fraction taken out in taxes from the last, or marginal, dollar of income earned.

Market-clearing, or equilibrium, price: The price that clears the market when there is no excess quantity demanded or supplied; the price at which the demand curve intersects the supply curve.

Market supply: Total quantities of a good offered for sale by suppliers at various prices.

Median age: The age that exactly separates the younger half of the population from the older half.

Minimum wage: A legal wage rate below which employers cannot pay workers.

Models, or theories: Simplified representations of the real world used to make predictions or to better understand the real world.

Monopolist: A single supplier.

Monopolistic competition: A market situation in which a large number of firms produce similar but not identical products, and in which there is relatively easy entry to the industry.

Monopoly: A firm that has great control over the price of a good. In the extreme case, a monopoly is the only seller of a good or service.

Monopsony: A single buyer:

Negative externality: A cost associated with an economic activity that is paid by third parties. Pollution is a negative externality.

Nominal interest rate: Defined as the rate of exchange between a dollar today and a dollar at some future time. For example, if the market, or nominal, rate of interest is 10 percent per year, then a dollar today can be exchanged for $1.10 one year from now; the market rate of interest.

Oligopoly: A market situation in which there are very few sellers and in which each seller knows that the other sellers will react to its changes in prices and quantities.

Opportunity cost: The highest-valued alternative that must be sacrificed to attain something or to satisfy a want.

Parity: A concept applied to the relative price of agricultural goods. The federal government has established parity by using a formula in which the price of agricultural goods was compared with the price of manufactured goods during the period 1910–1914. A parity price would give farmers the same relative price for their products (compared to what they buy) as they received during the period 1910–1914.

Portfolio: An assortment of stocks or bonds owned by an individual. Generally, the riskiness of a portfolio is lower than the riskiness of any of the individual stocks or bonds in the portfolio.

Preferred stock: A security that indicates financing obtained from investors by a corporation. Preferred stock is not a legal obligation for the firm and does not have a maturity, but pays a fixed dividend each year. It has preferred position over common stock, both for dividends and for assets in the event of the firm's liquidation.

Price elasticity of demand: The responsiveness of the quantity demanded for a commodity to a change in its price per unit. Price elasticity of demand is defined as the percentage change in quantity demanded divided by the percentage change in price.

Price elasticity of supply: The responsiveness of the quantity supplied of a commodity to a change in its price per unit. Price elasticity of supply is defined as the percentage change in quantity supplied divided by the percentage change in price.

Price support: A minimum price set by the government. To be effective, price supports must be coupled with a mechanism to rid the market of "surplus" goods that arise whenever the supported price is greater than the market-clearing price.

Profit: The income generated by selling something for a higher price than was paid for it. In production, the income generated is the difference between total revenues received from consumers who purchase the goods and the total cost of producing those goods.

Public information: Any kind of information that is widely available to the public.

Random walk: The situation in which future behavior cannot be predicted from past behavior. Stock prices follow a random walk.

Real interest rate: The rate of exchange between goods and services (real things) today and goods and services at some future date. The nominal rate of interest minus the inflation rate.

Recession: A period of time during which the rate of growth of business activity is consistently less than its long-term trend, or is negative.

Resource: An input used in the production of desired goods and services.

Saving: The unspent portion of a consumer's income, or the difference between a consumer's income and his or her consumption expenditures.

Scarcity: A reference to the fact that at any point in time there exists only a finite amount of resources—human and nonhuman. Scarcity of resources means that nature does not freely provide as much of everything as people want.

Share of stock: Legal claim to a share of the future profits of a corporation.

Shareholder: The owner of shares of stock.

Shortage: A situation in which an excess quantity is demanded or an insufficient quantity is supplied; the difference between the quantity demanded and the quantity supplied at a specific price below the market-clearing price.

Social cost: The full cost that society bears when a resource-using action occurs. For example, the social cost of driving a car is equal to all the private costs plus any additional cost that society bears (e.g., air pollution and traffic congestion).

Stock: The quantity of something at a point in time. An inventory of goods is a stock. A bank account at a point in time is a stock. Stocks are defined independent of time, although they are assessed at a point in time; savings are stock.

Subsidies: Negative taxes; payments to producers or consumers of a good or service. For example, farmers often get subsidies for producing wheat, corn, or peanuts.

Substitution effect: The change in the quantity of a good demanded that occurs when its price changes, holding income constant.

Superior good: A good on which consumers spend a rising share of their income as their income rises.

Supply curve: The graphic representation of the supply schedule; a line showing the supply schedule, which slopes upward (has a positive slope).

Supply schedule: A set of prices and the quantity supplied at each price; a schedule showing the rate of planned production at each relative price for a specified time period, usually one year.

Supply-side economics: A popular approach to economics in the early years of the Reagan administration ("Reaganomics"). Supply-siders maintain that an increase in the tax rate will cause a decrease in the amount of work (and income) within the economy; conversely, a decrease in the tax rate will cause an increase in the amount of work (and income) within the economy.

Surplus: An excess quantity supplied or an insufficient quantity demanded. The difference between the quantity supplied and the quantity demanded at a price above the market-clearing price.

Surtax: Literally, a tax upon a tax. If the regular rate on income is 20 percent, and a 50 percent surtax is imposed, this is equivalent to imposing an additional tax of 10 percent (20 percent $\times$ 50 percent) on income.

Tradeoff: A term relating to opportunity cost. In order to get a desired economic good, it is necessary to trade off some other desired economic good in a situation of scarcity. A tradeoff involves making a sacrifice in order to obtain something.

Union: An organization of workers that usually seeks to secure economic improvements for its members.

Value of marginal product: The change in total revenues that results from a unit change in a variable input; also equal to marginal physical product times marginal revenue, or MPP × MR.

Variable costs: Costs that vary with the rate of production. They include wages paid to workers, the cost of materials, and so on.

Index

Abortion
 costs, 42
 economics of, 40–48
Acquired immune deficiency
  syndrome (AIDS), 73
 prostitution and, 8–9
Acreage restriction programs,
  16–17
AIDS. *See* Acquired immune
  deficiency syndrome
Aid to Families with
  Dependent Children
  (AFDC), 200–201
Airline industry
 airports, 57–58, 61, 64–68
 air traffic control system,
  62–64
 delays, 57–68
 deregulation, 37–39, 59–61
 safety, 31–39
Airspace, pollution and, 166
Alaska, oil spill in, 151–152

Alcohol, 3
 "moonshine," 6
 product reliability, 9
 Prohibition-era penalties, 6–7
 taxation, 11–12
Algeria, wage rates, 131
American bison, 146
American Medical Association
  (AMA), 77–79
Amoco Cadiz, 152
Animals, extinct and
  endangered species,
  144–150
Aspirin, 73
Azidothymidine (AZT), 73–74

Banking, savings and loan
  associations, 91–98
Barley, 19
Benzene, 153
Beta blockers (drugs), 72

Blacks
　　erosion of family, 200–201
　　minimum wage and, 22–23
　　poverty among, 193–194
Bonds
　　definition of, 52
　　inside information, 56
　　price prediction, 55
Boulder (Colorado), water
　　usage, 27–28
Brazil, agricultural production,
　　18
Bribery, 12, 140
British Airports Authority, 67
Browning, Edgar, 196
Bubbles, pollution and, 166
Builders Emporium, 109
Bureaucracy, rent control and,
　　117
Burger, Warren E., 123
Burundi, elephant hunting in,
　　149
Bush, George, 21, 91, 98, 132,
　　203, 204

Cancer, smoking and, 220
Capital punishment, 171–174
Cartels, 50
　　international, 84–90
Central Selling Organization,
　　84, 89
Challenger space shuttle, 34n
China, agricultural production,
　　18
Chrysler Corporation, 97
CIPEC (Intergovernmental
　　Council of Copper
　　Exporting Countries),
　　87–88

Civil Aeronautics Board (CAB),
　　37–38, 58–60
Civil liberties, 124
Coca-Cola, 7n
Cocaine, 3, 6, 135, 136
　　deaths from use of, 10
　　manufacturing cost, 140
　　nature of usage, 7
　　price, 10
　　product reliability, 9–10
Cody, Bill, 146
Coffee, 88
Commodity Credit Corporation
　　(CCC), 16, 17
Common law, abortion and, 41
Common property, 134
　　clams and oysters as, 157–161
　　water as, 154
Competition
　　airline industry, 59–60
　　airline safety and, 37–38
　　in education, 208–210
　　illegal drugs and, 141–142
　　types of, 50
Constant quality units, supply
　　and demand and, 2
Construction, rent control and,
　　115–116
Consumer Price Index, 75
Contracts, enforcement of
　　illegal, 5–6
Copper, 87–88
Corn, acreage restriction
　　programs and, 16–17
Cost-benefit analysis
　　airline safety factors and,
　　32–33
　　capital punishment and,
　　172–173

Council of International Coffee
    Organizations (ICO), 88
Courts. *See also* Crime
    criminal convictions, 123
Coyotes, 150
Crime
    capital punishment, 171–174
    deterrents, 169–170
    murder, 171–174
    punishment and, 168–175
    social cost, 169
Crime prevention. *See also* Law
    enforcement
    economics of, 120–128
Criminals, evasion skills of, 5

DeBeers (corporation), 85–86,
    89
Demand
    elastic, 76*n*, 139
    law of, 2
Deregulation
    airline industry, 37–39, 59–61
    savings and loan industry, 94
Diamonds, 85–86, 89
Divorce, women and, 101–104
Drugs, illegal, 3
    addiction, 136*nn*
    consumer information, 7–8
    death rate, 10
    distribution, 6
    legal crackdown on
        suppliers, 4
    nature of usage, 7
    price, 10–11
    product reliability, 9–10
    retail value, 138
    risks and profit margins,
        139–140

social costs of war on,
    135–143
violence and, 5, 140–142
Drugs, medical, regulation of,
    69–74

Eastern buffalo, 146*n*
Ecology
    extinct and endangered
        species, 144–150
    income distribution and,
        185–189
    oil spills, 151–156
    property rights and
        economics of pollution,
        162–167
    wilderness preservation,
        187–188
Education, school economics,
    206–213
Eighteenth Amendment, 11
Elderly, 105–111
    Medicare. *See* Medicare
    per capita income, 106–107
    poverty among, 193–194
Elephants, 148–149
Endangered species, 144–150
Endangered Species Act, 144,
    149
Environmental impact
    statements, 149
Environmental Protection
    Agency (EPA), 164
Erlich, Isaac, 173–174
European lion, 146
Expansions, 87
Exports, agricultural products,
    18
Extinct species, 144–150

Exxon Corporation, 151–152, 154
Exxon Valdez, 151–153, 154

Fair Labor Standards Act, 21
Farms
  acreage restriction programs, 16–17
  divorce rate, 103–104
  exports, 18
  income distribution, 214–216
  payment-in-kind program, 18–19
  price supports, 14–19
  productivity and prosperity, 14
Farm Security Act, 18–19
Federal Aviation Administration (FAA), 35–36, 62–63, 67–68
Federal Bureau of Investigation (FBI), 169
Federal Clean Air Act, 164
Federal Deposit Insurance Corporation (FDIC), 92–93
Federal Home Loan Bank Board, 96
Federal Savings and Loan Insurance Corporation (FSLIC), 92–93, 94, 96
Federal Trade Commission (FTC), 60
Financial Institutions Reform, Recovery, and Enforcement Act, 91–92, 96
Flexner, Abraham, 77
Food and Drug Act, 69–70
Food and Drug Administration (FDA), 70, 72–74

Food, Drug, and Cosmetic Act, 70
Food for Peace program, 16
Free goods, 157–161

Gardner, B. Delworth, 29
General Mills, 13
Great Britain, airports in, 63–64, 67
Green Revolution, 18

Hanke, Steve, 27–28
Hashish, 7
Health
  pollution and, 162–163
  smoking and, 220
Heroin, 6, 7, 135, 136, 139
  deaths from use of, 10
Hitchings, George, 72
Hoskens, Bruce, 13
Housing
  government regulation and, 179–184
  rent control, 112–119
  vouchers, 203–204
Hovnanian, Ara K., 179
Hunting, 145, 146, 147–148

ICO (Council of International Coffee Organizations), 88
Illinois, pollution program in, 165
Immigrants, housing problems, 183–184
Impact fees, 182
Income distribution
  ecology and, 185–189
  government programs and, 214–218
Income effect, 131

Income elasticity of demand, 76*n*

Income mobility, 192–193

India, agricultural production, 18

Inside information, 56

Insurance
malpractice, 81
medical, 79–81

Intergovernmental Council of Copper Exporting Countries (CIPEC), 87–88

International Bauxite Association (IBC), 86

International Tin Agreement, 86

International Whaling Commission, 147–148

Jobs, minimum wage and loss of, 22

Job Training Partnership Act, 197, 202–203

Johnson, William, 196

Kefauver, Estes, 70

Kemp-Roth tax plan, 132

Kennedy, John F., 70

Knowles, Daniel, 108

Koch, Ed, 222

Law enforcement. *See also* Crime
crime prevention economics, 120–128
illegal drug users and, 6–7
police corruption, 140
social costs of drug wars, 135–143

and suppliers of illicit goods, 4

Layson, Stephen, 174

Licensing fees, 159

Loans, 94–95

Lockheed Corporation, 97

Marijuana, 6, 7, 135, 136, 139
product reliability, 9
profit margins, 140
supply and potency, 11

Maryland, oyster beds regulated in, 159–160

Median age, 105–106

Medicaid, 76, 191*n*

Medical costs
abortion, 42
insurance, 79–81
malpractice insurance, 81
physician salaries, 78
rise of, 75–83

Medicare, 76, 79, 107, 110, 193
payments, 106

Miami (Florida), prostitutes and AIDS rate in, 9

Mincer, Jacob, 23

Minimum wage, 20–24, 217
poverty and, 201–202

Minnesota
education system, 211–212
smoking legislation, 222

Minorities
abortion rate, 45
minimum wage and, 22–23
below poverty line, 199

Missouri, abortion statutes, 40*n*, 47

Mono Lake (California), 25–26

Mustang Ranch (Nevada), 8

National Aeronautics and Space Administration (NASA), 34n

National Air Quality Standards, 164

National Airspace System Plan, 63

National Assessment of Educational Progress (NAEP), 210

National Environmental Policy Act, 149

National Health Service (Great Britain), 107

National Research Council, 153

Nevada, prostitution legal in, 3, 8–9

Newark (New Jersey), prostitutes and AIDS rate in, 9

New Jersey, housing construction in, 179–180

Newport News (Virginia), crime prevention project in, 127–128

New York (city)
abortion rate, 45–46
criminal justice system, 123
drug enforcement in, 137–138
education system, 206–207
police budget, 120, 124
rent control in, 112–118
smoking legislation, 222
welfare hotels in, 198

New York (state), antiabortion statute in, 41

Nguyen Co Thach, 119

North Carolina, housing construction permits in, 180

Oats, 19
shortage, 13

Office of Thrift Supervision, 96, 97

Ogallala aquifer, 26

Oil
cartels and prices, 85–86
pollution, 151–156
price cuts, 89–90

Opium, 7

Orange (California), police salary program in, 126

Organization of Banana-Exporting Countries, 86

Organization of Petroleum Exporting Countries (OPEC), 85–86, 89–90

Ozone, 162–163

Pacific Southwest Airlines, 59n

Palmer, Arnold, 212

Passenger pigeon, 146

Payment-in-kind program, 18–19

Pennsylvania, pollution reduction in, 165

Per capita income, of elderly, 106–107

Phoenix (Arizona)
construction regulation in, 181
water usage, 26–27

Police. *See* Law enforcement

Pollution
emissions-trading schemes, 165–167
health hazards, 153
laws, 163–164
oil, 151–156
property rights and economics of, 162–167

visual, 185
water, 26
Polychlorinated biphenyls
    (PCBs), 163
Poverty
    changing face of, 198–205
    governmental in-kind
        transfers, 191*n*
    groups affected by, 193–194
    war on, 190–197
Poverty line
    elderly under, 107
    minimum wage and, 21–22
    population below, 190,
        198–199
Price, supply and demand and,
    2
Price supports, for farms, 14–19
Prisons
    construction costs, 169
    cost per inmate, 169
    population, 168
Production, factors of, 100
Prohibition era, 5, 6
    alcohol-related death rate
        during, 10
    bribery during, 12, 140
    failure of, 11
Property, common. *See*
    Common property
Prostitution, 11, 122–123
    health consequences and
        legality of, 8–9
    legal crackdown, 4
    legality in Nevada, 3

Quaker Oats Company, 13

Reagan, Ronald, 21, 129, 197,
    202, 203, 204

Recessions, 87
Rent control, 112–119, 217
Resolution Trust Corporation,
    96, 97
Retirement, 109–110
Roe v. Wade, 40, 42, 46, 47
Rosenbaum, James, 108
Rupp, Stewart, 164

Safety
    abortion, 42–43, 46
    airline, 31–39
Santa Barbara (California),
    water system hookup
    moratorium, 180
Santa Monica (California), rent
    control in, 112, 115–118
Saudi Arabia, agricultural
    surpluses, 18
Savings and loan associations,
    91–98
Scholastic Aptitude Test (SAT),
    210
Septra (drug), 72
Sherman, William Tecumseh,
    142
Slums, in affluent
    neighborhoods, 183–184
Smith, Adam, 170
Smoking, 219–223
Snail darter, 149–150
Social Security, 108, 109, 110,
    193
    payments, 106
Sorghum, acreage restriction
    programs and, 16–17
South Africa, elephant hunting
    in, 149
Soybeans, acreage restriction
    programs and, 16–17
Space shuttle, 34*n*

Stocks
definition of, 51–52
inside information, 56
price prediction, 53–54
random walk, 54–55
stockbrokers, 52–53
Summers, Lawrence, 23
Supply, law of, 2
Supply-side economics,
129–132
Supreme Court, abortion
decisions, 40–41, 42, 46, 47

Taxation, 129–132
alcohol, 11–12
drug addiction and, 136
of elderly, 109
and farm price supports, 16,
17
income distribution and,
216–217
law enforcement and, 125
progressive vs. proportional,
130
savings and loan associations
and, 91–92, 97–98
Social Security, 108, 109
tobacco and, 221
Tax Reform Act, 132
Teenagers, minimum wage,
22–23
Tennessee Valley Authority,
149–150
Thalidomide, 70
Third World, agricultural
production, 18
Times Mirror Company, 165
Tobacco, 219–223
Tucson (Arizona), water usage,
26–27

Venereal disease, prostitution
and, 8–9
Victims of Crime Act, 126–127
Violence
illegal contracts enforced by,
5–6
illegal drugs and, 140–141,
141–142
murder, 171–174
Virginia
smoking legislation, 222
tidal land ownership in, 160
Volkswagen, 165

Wages
income effect, 131
minimum, 20–24
Washington (state), clamming
regulations, 158–159
Water
moratorium on system
hookups, 180
pollution, 26
shortages, 25–30
*Webster v. Reproductive Health
Services*, 40–41, 42, 47
Welfare, 200–201, 204
Whales, 147–148
Wilderness preservation,
187–188
Women. *See also* Abortion
divorce and, 101–104
poverty among, 193–194, 199
Workers, low- and minimum-
wage, 20–24
Wright, Orville, 58
Wright, Wilbur, 58

Zimbabwe, elephant hunting
in, 149